GEORGE WASHINGTON'S

RULES OF CIVILITY

Complete with

the original French text

and new French-to-English

translations

by John T. Phillips, II

GEORGE WASHINGTON'S RULES OF CIVILITY

fourth revised
Collector's Classic Edition

THE COMPLEAT GEORGE WASHINGTON Series, Vol. I

Copyright 2003, 2006
Goose Creek Productions
Virginia Beach, Virginia

Phillips, John T., II.
        George Washington's rules of civility : complete with the
original French text and new French-to-English translations /
by John T. Phillips, II.-- 4th, collector's classic ed.; p. cm. --
    (The Compleat George Washington series; vol. 1)
    Includes bibliographic references and index.
    ISBN 09711173-22
    1. Washington, George, 1732-1799 -- Youth, education.
    2. Presidents, US -- George Washington. 3. Etiquette.
    I. Title: Rules of civility. II. Title. III. Series.

                3   5   7   9   11   12   10   8   6   4

Full cataloging information for this title is available from the
Library of Congress (U.S.) and the British Library (U.K.)

Printed in the United States of America
∞ acid-free papers and materials throughout ∞

Collector's Classic   (leather)   ISBN   978-09711173-27

TABLE OF CONTENTS

Origins of The Rules of Civility   7

Editorial Note   15

THE RULES OF CIVILITY

    General precepts
    Rules 1-24   19

    Duties in ceremony and conversation
    Rules 25-36   37

    Distinctions in rank among men
    Rules 37-50   52

    Clothing and apparel
    Rules 51-52   63

    Walking, alone or in company
    Rules 53-57   65

    Conversation, public and private
    Rules 58-89   72

    Table manners
    Rules 90-107   98

    Spiritual and moral
    Rules 108-110   113

Bibliography   117

Subject Index   121

ORIGINS OF THE RULES OF CIVILITY

In 1745, a thirteen year-old schoolboy in Virginia jotted down a lengthy set of social rules in his workbook. Like many other young men in the American colonies, young George Washington was learning how to conduct himself in the fashion of a respectable British gentleman. Following instruction, George titled his notes *The Rules of Civility*.

The rules of civility were not a colonial invention. Like today's rules of etiquette, the colonial rules of civility reflect hundreds of years of social and cultural changes in western civilization. Codes of chivalry were distant ancestors in the Middle Ages; more immediate forebears were visible in the parental advice and courtesy books of the Renaissance.

The Rules of Civility, in the form that George Washington learned them in 1745, follow maxims set out in a 1595 French manuscript titled *Bien-séance de la Conversation entre les Hommes*, ("Good Manners in Conversation among Men"). *Bien-séance*, which was generated by the Pensionnaires of the Jesuit College of La Flèche, then copied, translated and shared with Jesuits across Europe, was in essence the reorganized elaboration of an earlier Italian book, *Il Galateo*.

Around 1552, scholar and Catholic cleric Giovanni della Casa authored *Il Galateo*, a courtesy book that was eventually published after his death in 1556. Della Casa had been born into a patrician Florentine family in 1503. Early in life, he studied at several of the intellectual centers of northern Italy - Bologna, Padua and Florence - and in Rome. Della Casa's studies gave him a solid footing in the intellectual movement that is now known as Renaissance humanism.

Through political connections within the Catholic church, della Casa obtained appointments under Popes Paul III and Paul IV, serving as the Archbishop of Benevento and later as the Papal Nuncio to Venice. During the period of della Casa's ascendancy in the church, Paul III founded the Society of Jesus ("Jesuits"), one of the Catholic responses to the then-new, surging Protestant Reformation. Giovanni della Casa was a visible church figure, formulating and implementing Catholic reactions to the Reformation that included establishment of the Inquisition in Venice and the compilation of a Roman *Index of Prohibited Books*. Della Casa's *Il Galateo* would have been both familiar to and influential with members of the Jesuit order.

Il Galateo was written in a narrative prose; della Casa borrowed from classical sources, particularly Aristotle and Cicero. Forty years later, in generating *Bien-séance*, the Jesuits at La Flèche eliminated most of the parables from *Il Galateo* and reorganized the subject matter into distinct situational groupings. By the end of the 16th Century, Jesuits were educating the children of the nobility all over Continental Europe, and deportment was an increasingly important subject. In order to obtain a wider readership for *Bien-séance*, the Bishop of Toul commissioned Jesuit scholar Léonard Périn to translate the rules into Latin. Périn added new rules regulating table manners, and his manuscript, titled *Les Maximes de la Gentillesse et de l'Honnesteté en la Conversation entre les Hommes*, was published in 1617. In 1629, a German printer named

Joannes Nitzmann published the Rosetta Stone of *Bien-séance*, setting Périn's Latin and German and Bohemian translations of Périn in parallel columns. These same maxims were also translated into Spanish. Thus, *Bien-séance* was providing a uniform set of social ideals for the early modern European sub-cultures in the 1630s, at the very same time that both political and commercial life in Europe was reorienting in and around increasingly urban environs.

The first English version of the rules of civility, a translation of della Casa's *Il Galateo* titled *A Treatise of Maners*, was printed in London in 1576. Similarly, two decades after its publication in Latin, Périn's *Les Maximes* was translated into English and appeared in London in 1641, titled *Youth's Behaviour, or Decency in Conversation amongst men*. An eight year-old, Francis Hawkins, was credited with the translation although his youthful age may have been exploited by his family for the sake of marketing of the book. Francis' uncle Henry Hawkins was a prominent Jesuit scholar and translator, and his father Dr. John Hawkins, and another uncle Sir Thomas Hawkins, were both also notorious (in Anglican England) for their translations of Catholic texts. Francis Hawkins joined the Jesuit order in 1649, and by the time the tenth English edition of *Youth's Behaviour* was published 1672 he was serving as the Jesuit Confessor of Ghent.

A copy of *Youth's Behaviour* would be utilized by George Washington's teacher as his text for the rules. Coincidentally, a 1664 version of *Youth's Behaviour* contained a supplemental "Second Part," by Robert Codrington, dedicated to the heiress of one Laurence Washington, Esq., "of Garsden," who had died in 1662.

This Second Part dealt exclusively with "Conversation Amongst Women." There is, however, absolutely no evidence that George Washington learned from or ever knew of the existence of the 1664 edition.

In 1663, the maxims were edited and revised by Pierre de Bresche, of Clermont Jesuit College in Paris, who translated Périn's Latin back into French, adding new epicurean instructions in the process. In 1673, an "anonymous" French edition based on Hawkins (it included Codrington's Second Part rules for women), was published in Paris. This French volume was then "translated" and published in English in 1678.

In the meanwhile, Antoine de Courtin published *Nouveau traité de la civilité* in Paris in 1670. Courtin's book contained an exceptionally detailed set of rules, but essentially just expanded on *Bien-séance*. Courtin's book was translated into English in 1671, and titled *The Rules of Civility*. This is the first use of the title that George Washington would enter in his notebook.

Which brings us back to George Washington. In 1745 in Fredericksburg Virginia, a colonial town near the frontier of the British empire, George Washington learned and recorded *The Rules of Civility*.

Because the Washington family was relatively prosperous, young George had been fortunate enough to attend several schools, beginning when he was seven. At the first school George attended, in a cabin near Falmouth Church, "Hobby" Grove, the church sexton, taught the basics of reading and writing. Business and legal forms were introduced into young George's studies at the age of nine. After all, a Virginia planter could not function properly without some knowledge of contracts and the law. When George was ten, he was presented with an instructional workbook, *The Young Man's Companion*. This all-in-one manual supplied various business forms, and lessons in construction, surveying and navigation at sea.

George's father and his two older half-brothers, Lawrence and Augustine, had all attended Appleby school in England and George had every prospect of following them in the family tradition. However, when George was eleven, his father died suddenly and young George's options were altered dramatically. Instead of going off to England for schooling, George's mother urged him stay in Virginia and pursue an occupation that would generate an income. So, when George was twelve, he went to live with his older brother Augustine, at the traditional Washington family home on Pope's Creek, while he attended Henry Williams' school at Laurel Grove in Westmoreland County. At that time, George began his formal studies of mathematics, business and the practice of surveying, which would eventually become his first occupation.

In 1745, George returned to "Ferry Farm," the property he had inherited across the Rappahannock from Fredericksburg, where his mother and younger siblings were living. The evidence that is available suggests that George lived at both Ferry Farm and Mt. Vernon during each of the next several years, and that he was briefly enrolled in the classical high school of instruction led by the Rev. James Marye.

Reverend Marye, rector of St. George's Church in Fredericksburg from 1735 to 1767, taught mathematics, Latin and deportment. Between visits to his brother Lawrence at Mt. Vernon and his Washington cousins in Chotank, George studied under the guidance of Rev. Marye. Marye had been born and raised in Rouen, France, and had studied in the Jesuit College of Rouen before renouncing the Catholic faith in 1726, fleeing to England, and taking up Anglican orders. During his first year of study with Rev. Marye, George Washington learned and wrote down his manuscript (MS) version of what we now know as *The Rules of Civility*. Examination of the notebook reveals a manuscript written in a sometimes hurried colonial shorthand, leading one to conclude that George took the rules in dictation, as if in a lecture, and that he did not simply copy them from some unknown text.

Comparing Washington's MS with earlier French and Hawkins texts leads to conflicting conclusions about their origins. It appears that a late version of Hawkins, (but not the 1664 edition), gave outline form to the MS. This conclusion is supported by the sequential reiteration of "additional" and "appendix" Hawkins rules, while eighteen of the rules appear to have no reference in the French maxims but rather derive from Hawkins, and errors in the Hawkins text, (see Rule #8), are repeated in the MS. However, in several instances, (for example, Rules #45, #52 and #106), the MS clearly follow French maxims, and not Hawkins. Also, the Hawkins text is only used selectively and seldom repeated verbatim, while structures of French idioms are recurrent throughout the Washington MS. A fair linguistic analysis leads one to conclude that George's instruction in the rules incorporated English translations of French phrases. To his embarrassment as an adult, George Washington never learned French. George's instructor evidently

Origins of the

possessed a fundamental knowledge of the French maxims but used Hawkins as his lecture guide.

The workbook that contained the Washington MS sat relatively undisturbed for nearly a century, aside from the unwanted attention of some inquisitive mice, until Washington's private papers were purchased for the Library of Congress in 1849. By then, George Washington's biographers had begun to explore the history of *The Rules of Civility*. The notorious Jared Sparks made a first, inaccurate use of the Washington MS. Later writers, like Washington Irving, invented a "homespun" origin for the MS, thus misrepresenting or ignoring George Washington's formal schooling.

The 1880s proved to be a decade of intense scholarship in the subject of etiquette. A manual titled *Of Education. Especially of Young Gentlemen*, the work of Obadiah Walker, Master of the University College at Oxford, was published in England in 1887. Walker generally followed Périn's version of the French maxims, without citing him or them. On the American side of the Atlantic, J.M. Toner published his transcript of the Washington MS, titled *George Washington's Rules of Civility & Decent Behaviour in Company and Conversation*. Dr. Toner's 1888 work finally revealed the full surviving text of the MS, including shorthand abbreviations, original capitalization, odd punctuation and spelling, and typos, leaving unfilled gaps where mice and time had eaten away at the pages; (literally dozens of the rules had been partially obliterated).

In 1890, renowned author and theologian Moncure Conway, who had attended Fredericksburg Academy in the 1840s, followed Toner with his ground-breaking work, *George Washington's Rules of Civility*. Conway traced *The Rules of Civility* to their several sources, identifying the early European versions of the rules, explaining origins and interrelationships of the various editions, and supplementing Toner's work by filling in the missing text in George Washington's MS. Conway also marshalled evidence and originated the notion that the former French Jesuit-turned-Anglican Rev. Marye instructed George Washington in the rules.

Ever since 1926, academics and pundits alike have afforded undue credence to author Charles Moore's arbitrary, unjustified dismissal of Moncure Conway's scholarship. Curiously uninformed and blinded, recent works on *The Rules of Civility* have continued to follow Moore's inaccurate, agenda-driven "reconstructions" of the Washington MS, in the process losing sight of two important facets of the bigger picture.

The first is the remarkable hand of the Jesuits in *The Rules of Civility*, connecting Giovanni della Casa in Renaissance Italy, to the scholars of the Jesuit colleges across Europe, to the Hawkins family of London, to the Rev. James Marye in Fredericksburg, Virginia.

Of far greater importance, the codes of chivalry of the Middle Ages, courtesy and advice books of the Renaissance, metropolitan civility of Washington's colonial times and today's etiquette all occupy vital places on our cultural continuum. In studying the rules of civility today we revisit the role that codes of conduct have had in the maturation of civilization, and we revitalize our personal connection to that past.

So imagine, now, that you are in school once again, sitting next to George Washington, a thirteen year-old gentleman in training, working hard at improving himself, learning to abide by *The Rules of Civility*.

Origins of the

EDITORIAL NOTE

The following text is composed of four distinct elements, with each originating in a different century. Accordingly, the editorial approach to each element is unique unto itself.

George Washington's manuscript (MS) version, circa 1745, is emphasized and presented in over-sized type. I edited the MS with the intent of retaining the full sense and feel of it's colonial American origin. The Washington MS was written in a colonial short-hand, evidently with some haste, as if young George was taking dictation or rapidly making notes during a lecture. I restore his text to full sentences, and correct grammar, capitalization and punctuation. However, archaic colonial spellings are not changed if they will not confuse the modern reader. For example, his use of "arrogancy," "inferiour," "ye" and "'tis" were acceptable in George Washington's time and are still perfectly understood today. I present corrections of significant, long-standing misinterpretations of the Washington MS in Rules #67 and #78.

The French language text is archaic middle French, derived from a copy of de Bresche's 1663 French and Latin edition [cited as "Maxims"] that now resides in the King George III Collection at the British Library. The French has been edited for consistency; archaic spelling and inflection marks are retained whenever the derivative modern French word is apparent. I rely upon Moncure Conway for his reconstruction of the original French maxims and initial translations, and for his revelations of the French and English works of the 1600s and 1800s that built upon or revised the French maxims. While Conway's translations and commentary are completely overhauled, his work has provided the spark of inspiration for the tome in hand.

Revised modern English translations of the French texts from the 1600s are presented in italics. The Francis "Hawkins" translations of 1640, published as *Youth's Behaviour*, are also presented in italics.

In my commentaries, I attempt to limit my remarks to the elaboration of significant sources and alternate interpretations. I quote the Eisenbichler and Bartlett translations of Giovanni della Casa's 1552 text [cited as "*Galateo*"]. Comments referring to the "original French" cite the 1595 work of the Pensionnaires of La Flèche; the "anonymous French" text is a reference to the revised 1673 edition. "Walker" is a reference to Obadiah Walker's 1887 book, *Of Education*. "Dr. Toner" refers to J.M. Toner's 1888 transcript of the Washington MS. I also refer to two contemporary versions of The Rules of Civility, the 2002 edition by "Mt. Vernon" and a revised 1997 version by Richard "Brookhiser." Finally, I trust that my Subject Index to the Rules will prove itself a useful contribution.

This work was advanced with, and my thanks to, assistance from: the professional staffs of the British Library in London England, the library at George Washington's Mt. Vernon, the Library of Congress, and, the Alderman library in Charlottesville Virginia; my former colleague at the University of Virginia, Stephen Siu-Kay On - with his English interpretations of the middle French texts; and, Michael Embrey - with the splendid illustrations of colonial life.

RULES OF CIVILITY

&

DECENT BEHAVIOUR

IN COMPANY

AND CONVERSATION

1st: Every action done in company ought to be with some sign of respect to those that are present.

Que toutes actions qui se font publiquement fassent voir son sentiment respectueux à toute la compagnie. [Maxims, II-1]

Let all actions performed in public show some sign of respectful sentiment to the entire company.

2d: When in company, put not your hands to any part of the body that is not usually discovered.

Gardez-vous bien de toucher de la main aucune partie de vostre corps, de celles qui ne sont poinct en veuë, en la presence d'aucune autre personne. Pour les mains, & le visage, cela leur est ordinaire. Et afin de vous y accoustumer pratiquez ce poinet de civilité mesme en vostre particulier. [Maxims, II-3]

When in the presence of others, refrain from touching any part of the body that is not usually within view. The hands and face are ordinarily visible. In order to form the habit in this point of etiquette, practice it when you are with your intimate friends.

3ᵈ: Show nothing to your friend
      that may affright him.

    Ne faites pas voir à vostre compagnon, ce qui luy pourroit faire mal au coeur. [Maxims, II-4]

    Show nothing to your companion that may grieve him, since that might provoke a misunderstanding.

4ᵗʰ: In the presence of others, sing not
       to yourself with a humming noise;
       nor drum with your fingers or feet.

    Ne vous amusez pas à chanter en vous mesme, si vous ne vous rencontrez si fort à l'écart qu'aucun autre ne vous puisse entendre; non plus qu'à contre-faire le son du tambour par l'agitation des pieds ou des mains. [Maxims, II-5]

    Do not seek amusement by singing to yourself, unless you are beyond the hearing of others; do not tap out the beat of a drum with your hands or feet.

    In 1552, Giovanni della Casa advises his readers not to indulge in "humming to oneself, or tapping one's fingers, or moving one's leg to and fro," because these are the actions of an inconsiderate person. [*Galateo*, Chap. 6]

5th: If you cough, sneeze, sigh or yawn, do it not loud, but privately; and speak not in your yawning, but put your handkerchief or hand before your face and turn aside.

Quand vous toussez ou quand vous ésternuez, si vous pouvez estre le maistre de ces efforts de nature, n'éclatez pas si hautement & si fort. Ne poussez pas des soûpirs si aigres que les autres les puissent entendre. [Maxims, II-8]

Whenever you cough or sneeze, if you can control these natural efforts, do not sound off so highly or loudly. Do not heave sighs so noisily that others hear.

Ne soufflez pas si asprement, faisant des hurlements en baaillant. Et s'il vous est possible, empeschez vous absolumēt de baailler; mais ayez en un bien plus grand soin, quand vous vous entretenez avec quelqu'un, ou dans quelque conversation. Car c'est un signe manifest d'un certain dégoust de ceux avec quivous. Si vous ne vous pouvez pas empescher de baailler, du moins gardez-vous bien de parler en cet instant mesme, & d'ouvrir extraordin-airemēt la bouche; mais pressez la sagement, ou en détournant tant soi peu la face de la cōpagnie. [Maxims, II-9]

When you yawn, refrain from howling. If you can, avoid yawning altogether when you are in company or engaged in conversation. For it is a clear sign of a

certain weariness with those about you. If you cannot
stop from yawning, avoid gaping widely and also
refrain from speaking while doing. Also press at your
mouth adroitly or turn a little away from the company.

According to Moncure Conway, the anonymous
1673 French work advises one: "in sneezing, not to
shake the foundations of the house."

6th:   Sleep not when others speak.
        Sit not when others stand. Speak not
        when you should hold your peace.
        Walk not when others stop.

C'est une incivilité & une impertinence de
dormir, pendant que la cõpagnie s'entretient de
discours; de se tenir assis lors que tout le monde est
débout, de se promener lors que personne ne branle,
& de parler quád il est temps de se taire ou
d'écouter. Pour celuy touttesfois qui a l'authorité, il
y a des temps & des lieux où il luy est permis de se
promener seul, comme à un Precepteur qui est dans
la classe. [Maxims, II-11]

It is an affront and an impertinence to doze while
everyone is engaged in conversation, to be seated while
the rest stand, to walk on while others pause, or to
speak when you should be silent or listen. For those in
authority, such as a Master in his classroom, there are
times and places when it is admissible to walk alone.

7th: Put not off your cloths in the
         presence of others, nor go out
         of your chamber half dressed.

Il n'est pas séant d'avoir son lict en mauvais
ordre dans sa chābre, non plus que de s'habiller en
la presence des autres, ou de s'y dépoüiller, ou de
sortir de sa mesme chābre à demy habillé, couvert
de sa coiffe, ou de son bonnet-de-nuict, de rester
débout en sa chābre ou estre attaché à son pulpitre
avec sa robe ouverté. Et quoy que vous ne
manquiez pas de serviteur qui prenne le soin de faire
vostre lict; toutes-fois en sortant, prenez garde de le
laisser découvert. [Maxims, II-12]

*It is not becoming to leave your room while your
bed is in disorder, or to dress or undress in the presence
of others, or to leave your bedroom half-dressed, half-
groomed or wearing your night-cap, or to remain
standing in your chamber or at your desk in an open
gown. And, although you may have servants to make
your bed; nevertheless, take care when you go out of
your chamber not to leave your bed uncovered.*

8th: At play and at fire, it is good
         manners to give a place to the
         last comer; and affect not to
         speak louder than ordinary.

Il est mal-séante, dans le jeu, ou aupres du feu de faire attendre trop long-temps ceux qui viennent à s'y presenter. [Maxims, II-15]

It is bad manners at play, and at the fireside, to make a new-comer wait very long for a place.

Prenez garde de vous échauffer trop au jeu, & aux emportements qui s'y éleuēt ... [Maxims, II-16]

Guard against becoming overheated at play, and that its excitements do not carry you away ...

George Washington's teacher, in equating excitement with loud speech, apparently followed Hawkins in a misinterpretation of Maxim #II-16.

9th: Spit not in the fire, nor stoop low before it. Neither put your hands into the flames to warm them, nor set your feet on the fire, especially if there be meat before it.

C'est une action peu hōneste de cracher dans la cheminée, d'approcher ses m̄ains trop prés de la flâme pour les échauffer, & de les mettre même dedans, de se baisser devāt le feu, comme si l'on éstoit assis à terre & s'y tenir courbé; s'il arrive qu'il y ait quelque chose devāt le feu, à cuire, prenez bien garde d'éstendre le pied pardessus le feu.

"GUARD AGAINST BECOMING OVERHEATED
AT PLAY ... THAT ITS EXCITEMENTS
DO NOT CARRY YOU AWAY ..."

Dans une honneste compagnie n'y tournez iamais le
dos, & ne vous en approchez point plus prés que les
autres - car ce sont des privilèges de personnes
qualifiées. Quand il n'en est point besoin, de
remuer le feu, y pousser le bois, l'y fourrer plus
avant ou l'en lever, il n'appartient qu'à celuy qui doit
avoir le soin de tout ce qui est à faire.
[Maxims, II-17]

*It is a crude action to spit in the fireplace, to hold
the hands too close to the flame in warming them, or
to crouch in front of the fire as if sitting on the ground;
if something is being cooked on the fire, do not extend
your foot over it. In polite society, do not turn your
back to the fire and do not approach it closer than
others - for these are the privileges of persons of rank.
When there is a need for stirring the fire, putting wood
on or pulling or lifting it, this is the job of the person
who has the general superintendence of those things.*

10th:   When you sit down, keep your
          feet firm on the ground and
          even, without putting one foot
          on the other or crossing them.

Pour l'ordre que l'on doit tenir étant assis, c'est
de placer bien ses pieds à terre en égale distãce que
les cuisses, non pas de crosier une cuisse ou un pied
sur l'autre. [Maxims, II-18]

*When seated, place your feet firmly on the ground,
with the legs at an equal distance, and neither a leg
nor a foot should be crossed one upon the other.*

Giovanni della Casa is silent on the subject of
seated posture, leaving one to conclude that this rule
reflects a code of behaviour that was typical of Jesuit
schoolrooms of the late sixteenth Century.

11th: Shift not yourself in the sight of others, nor gnaw your nails.

C'est une incivilité insupportable d'allonger son corps en estendant les bras, ou de faire différents postures. [Maxims, II-7]

When in public, it is an insufferable breach of etiquette to stretch out one's body by extending the arms, or to assume different postures.

Il ne faut iamais rogner ses ongles dans le public; & bien moins les prendre à belles dents. [Maxims, II-19]

It is absolutely forbidden to pare your nails in public, and also do not gnaw your nails.

12th: Shake not the head, feet, or legs. Roll not the eyes, lift not one eyebrow higher than the other. Wry not the mouth, and bedew no man's face with your spittle by approaching too near when you speak.

Vous ne hocherez point la teste, vous ne remuerez point les jambes, ny ne roüillerez les yeux, ne froncerez point les sourcils, ou tordrez la bouche. Vous vous garderez de laisser aller avec vos paroles

de la salive, ou du crachat aux visages de ceux, avec qui vous conversez. Pour obvier à cét accident, vous ne vous en approcherez point si prés; mais vous les entretiendrez dans une distãce raisonnable.
[Maxims, II-21]

Do not shake the head, nor fidget the legs, nor roll the eyes, nor frown, nor twist the mouth. Take care not to let saliva escape with your words, and do not let spittle fly into the faces of those with whom you converse. To prevent such an accident, do not approach your conversant too near; but engage in conversation at a reasonable distance.

13th: Kill no vermin such as fleas, lice, ticks, & etc., in the sight of others. If you see any filth or thick spittle, put your foot dexterously upon it. If it be upon the clothes of your companions, put it off privately, and if it be upon your own clothes return thanks to him who puts it off.

Gardez-vous bien de vous arrester, à tuër une puce, ou quelque sale bestiole de cette espece, en presence de qui que ce puisse estre. Que si quelque chose d'immõde vient à vous offenser la veuë, en regardant à terre, comme quelque crachat infect, ou quelqu' autre chose semblable, mettez-le pied dessus. S'il en attache quelqu' une aux habits de celuy à qui vous parlez, ou voltige dessus, gardez-vouz bien de la luy monstrer, ou à quelqu' autre personne; mais travaillez autant que vous pourrez à l'oster adroitement. Et s'il arrive que quelqu' un vous oblige tant que de vous défaire de quelque chose de semblable; faites luy paroistre vostre reconnoissance. [Maxims, II-22]

Do not stop to kill lice or any other disgusting animals of this kind in the presence of your company. If anything on the ground, such as phlegm or spittle, offends the sight, then put your foot on it. If it is on the garment of someone with whom you are conversing, do not show it to him or to anyone else, but do your best to remove it unobserved. If someone obliges you in this way, make your acknowledgments to him.

14th: Turn not your back to others, especially in speaking. Jog not the table or desk on which another reads or writes. Lean not upon anyone.

En la recontre que l'on fait des personnes, quand on les entretient, c'est une chose mal-séante de leur tourner le dos & les épaules. C'est une action impertinente de heurter la table ou d'ébranler le pupitre, dont un autre se sert pour lire, ou pour écrire. C'est une incivilité de s'appuyer sur quelqu' un, de tirer sa robbe, lors que l'on luy parle ou que l'on le peut entretenir. [Maxims, II-24]

When you are being introduced to people, and while speaking to them, it is very bad manners to turn your back and shoulders. It is an impertinent act to disturb the table or shake the desk that another person is using for reading or writing. It is uncivil to lean against anyone, or to pull at anyone's clothes, while you entertain them in conversation.

15ᵗʰ: Keep nails clean and short, and your hands and teeth clean, yet without showing any concern for them.

Gardez-vous bien de vous arrester en toute sorte de conversation, à rajuster vostre rabat, ou à rehausser vos chausses pour les faire joindre & en paroître plus galand. Que vous ongles ne soient point rēplis d'ordures, ny trop longs. Ayez grand soin de la netteté de vos mains; mais n'y recherchez point la volupté. [Maxims, II-25]

Take good care not to stop, in any sort of conversation, to adjust the garters for your leggings, or to pull up your stockings to make them join and thus appear more gallant. Do not allow your nails to be full of dirt, or too long. Take great care for the cleanliness of your hands, but do not over-do it.

Hawkins, our young London "translator," puts it: "without overmuch attendance thereon, or curiosity."

16th: Do not puff up the cheeks, loll not out the tongue; [do not] rub the hands or beard, thrust out the lips or bite them, or keep the lips too open or too close.

C'est une vilainie de s'enfler les joües, de tirer la langue, de se manier la barbe, se frotter les mains, d'éstendre ses lèvres ou les mordre, de les tenir trop serrées ou trop entrouvertes. [Maxims, II-26]

It is a very low act to puff up the cheeks, to stick out the tongue, to pull on one's beard, to rub one's hands, to chew or bite on the lips, or to hold the mouth too widely open or too tightly closed.

17th: Be no flatterer; neither play with any that delight not to be played with.

Ne flattez & n'amadoüez personne par belles parloes, car celui qui pretend d'en gagner un autre par les discours emmiellez, fait voir qu'il n'en à pas grande estime, & qu'il le tient pour peu sensé & adroit, dés qu'il le prend pour un hōme que l'on peut joüer en cette manière. N'usez point de gausseries auprés d'une personne qui s'en offense. [Maxims, II-27]

Do not flatter or wheedle anyone with fair words, for he who aspires to gain another's favor by his honied words shows that the speaker does not regard him in high esteem, and that the speaker deems him far from sensible or clever, in taking him for a man who may be tricked in this manner. Do not play practical jokes on those who would take as an offense.

18th: Read no letters, books or papers in company; but when there is a necessity for doing so, you must ask leave. Come not near the books or writings of another, so as to read them, unless desired; nor give your opinion of them unasked. Also look not when another is writing a letter.

C'est une action directement opposée à la bienséance, de lire quelque livre, quelques lettres ou autres choses semblables dans une conversation ordinaire, si ce n'est en une affaire pressante, ou pour quelque peu de moments; & mesme encore en ce cas, est-il à propos d'en demãder la permission, si vous n'êstes, possible, le Superieur de la compagnie. C'est encore pis de manier les ouvrages des autres, leurs livres, & d'autres choses de cette nature, de s'y attacher, d'en approcher la veuë de plus prés, sans la permission de celuy à qui la chose apparient, aussi bien que de leur donner des loüanges, ou les censurer, avant que l'on vous en demande vostre sentiment; de s'approcher trop prés, & d'incommoder celuy de qui ou est voisin, lors qu'il prend la lecture de ses letteres ou de quelqu' autre chose. [Maxims, II-28]

It is an act directly opposed to good manners to read a book, letters, or similar thing during ordinary conversation if it is not a pressing matter, or resolved very quickly; and even in that case, it is proper to ask permission unless you are, possibly, the highest in rank of the company. It is even worse to handle other people's work, their books or things of that nature, to get too near to these objects, to look at them closely without the owner's permission, and also to praise or find fault with them before your opinion has been asked; or to approach to close and inconvenience anyone when he is reading his letters or other papers.

19th:   Let your countenance be pleasant, but in serious matters somewhat grave.

Que le visage ne paroisse point fantastique, changeant, égaré, rauy en admiration, couvert de tristesse, divers & volage, & ne fasse paraître aucun signe d'un esprit inquiet. Au contraire, qu'il soit ouvert & tranquille, mais qu'il ne soit pas trop épanoüy de joye dans les affaires sérieuses, ny trop retiré par une grauité affectée dans la conversation ordinaire & familière de la vie humaine.
[Maxims, II-29]

The face should not look fantastic, changeable, absent, rapt in admiration, covered with sadness, various or volatile; and it should not show any signs of an unquiet mind. On the contrary, it should be open and tranquil, but not too expansive with joy in serious affairs, nor too self-contained by an affected gravity in the ordinary and familiar conversation of human life.

BRADDOCK'S DEFEAT, 1755.

20th: The gestures of the body must be suited to the discourse you are upon.

Let the gestures of thy body be agreeable to the matter of thy discourse. For it hath been ever held a solaesime [sic - solecism] in oratory to point to the Earth when thou talks of Heaven. [Hawkins, I-30]

Conway notes that the Maxim closest to Rule #20 directs: "Parmy les discours regardez à mettre vostre corps en belle posture." Or, "that, while speaking be careful to assume an elegant posture."

21st: Reproach none for the infirmities of nature, nor delight to put them that have infirmities in mind thereof.

Ne reprochez les défauts à personne. Non pas mesme de la nature, & ne prenez plaisir à faire confusion à qui que ce soit, par vos paroles. [Maxims, IV-6]

Reproach none for their infirmities. Avoid it equally when they are natural ones, and do not take pleasure in uttering words that cause anyone shame, whoever it may be.

22d: Show not yourself glad at the misfortune of another, though he were your enemy.

When thou shalt hear the misfortunes of another, shew not thy self gladdened for it, though it happens to thy enemy; for that will argue a mind mischievous, and will convict thee of a desire to have executed it thy self, had either power or opportunity seconded thy will. [Hawkins, I-32]

Conway does not find anything in the Maxims corresponding to Rule #22. The anonymous French work has: "Do not show yourself joyful and pleased at the misfortunes that have befallen another, though you hated him - it argues a mischievous mind, that you had a desire to have done it yourself, and if you had the power or opportunity to, you would have."

23^{d}:   When you see a crime punished, you may be inwardly pleased; but always show pity to the suffering offender.

When thou sees justice executed on any, thou may inwardly take delight in his vigilancy, to punish offenders because it tends to public quiet. Yet show pity to the offender, and ever constitute the defect of his morality as thy precaution. [Hawkins, I-33]

24th: Do not laugh too loud or too much at any public spectacle lest you cause yourself to be laughed at.

Laugh not too much or too loud, in any public spectacle least, for so doing, thou present thy self the only thing worthy to be laughed at. [Hawkins, I-34]

25th: Superfluous complements and all affectation of ceremony are to be avoided; yet where due they are not to be neglected.

Quoy qu'il soit bon de s'épargner un trop grand soin de pratiquer une civilité affectée, il faut pourtant estre exact à en observer ce qui est necessaire & avantageux pour faire paroistre une belle éducation, & ce qui ne se peut obmettre sans choquer ceux avec qui l'on converse.
[Maxims, III-1]

Though it is right to avoid too great of a care in practicing an affected civility, one must be exact in observing the social forms that are necessary and advantageous to show a good education, and all that are not should be omitted without shocking one's conversants.

26th:   In pulling off your hat to persons of distinction, such as noblemen, justices, churchmen & etc., make a reverence; bowing more or less according to the custom of the better bred and quality of persons. Amongst equals, expect not always that they should begin with you first; but to pull off the hat when there is no need is affectation. In the manner of saluting and re-saluting in words, keep to the most usual custom.

Témoignez vos respects aux hōmes illustres & honorables, le chappeau en la main, comme aux

Ecclesiastiques, ou aux Magistrats, ou à quelques autres personnes qualifiées; en tenant vers vous le dedans du chappeau que vous aurez osté. Faites leur aussi la reverence par quelque inclination de corps, autant que la dignité de chacun d'eux, & la belle coûtume des enfants bien nourris, le semble exiger. Et comme c'est une chose fort incivile de ne se pas découvrir devāt ceux à qui l'on doit ce respect, pour les saluër, ou d'attendre que vostre égal vous rende le premier ce devoir; aussi de la faire, quand il n'est pas à propos, ressēt sa civilité affectée; mais c'est une honteuse impertinence de prendre garde si l'on vous rend vostre salutation. Au reste pour saluër quelqu' un de parole, ce compliment semble le plus propre, qui est usité par personnes le plus polies. [Maxims, III-2]

Show your respect, hat in hand, for illustrious and honorable men such as church officials, Magistrates or other persons of quality; holding the inside of your removed hat towards you. Make your reverence to them by inclining your body as much as the dignity of each and the custom of well-bred youth seems to demand. It is very rude not to uncover the head before those to whom one owes such respect in order to salute them, or to wait till your equal should perform this duty towards you first; also, doffing one's hat when it is not fitting savours of affected politeness; but it is a shameful impertinence to be anxious for the return of one's salute. Finally, it seems most fitting to salute anyone in words, with a compliment which the most polite persons are in the habit of using.

27th: Tis ill manners to bid one more
eminent than yourself be covered, as
well as not to do it to whom it's due.
Likewise, he that makes too much
haste to put on his hat does not well,
yet he ought to put it on at the first,
or at most the second time of being
asked. Now, what is herein spoken, of
qualification in behaviour in saluting,
ought also to be observed in the
taking of place, and sitting down for
ceremonies which, without bounds, is
troublesome.

C'est une grande incivilité d'entreprendre de
prier un superieur de se couvrir, aussi bien que de
n'en pas supplier celuy à qui cela se peut faire. Et
celuy qui se haste trop de se couvrir, particuliérement en parlãt à quelque personne qualifiée, ou qui
pressé par plusieurs fois de ce faire, le refuse,
choque la bien-séance. C'est pour cela qu'à la une
ou deaux fois il est permis de se couvrir, si l'usage ne
se trouve contraire en quelque Province ou
Royaume. Et en effet entre les égaux, ou avec de
plus âgez, soit Religieux, ou domestiques, il est
permis d'accorder cette requeste à un égal ou à un
plus jeune, dés la première fois. Toutefois ceux qui
sõt égaux, ou fort peu différents les uns des autres,
ont coustume de se faire cette priere, & de se
couvrir tout ensemble. Toutes les remarques dõc
qui se sont faites icy de la bonne cõduite, doivent

George Washington's

estre aussi entenduës de l'ordre qu'il faut tenir à prendre place, & à s'asseoir; car le plasisir que l'on prend aux civilitez & aux complimēs, est tout à fait importun. [Maxims, III-3]

It is great breach of etiquette to ask a superior to be covered, just as it is not to do so in the case of one for whom asking it is proper. And the man who is in haste to put his hat on, especially when talking to a person of quality, or who, having been urged several times to do so, refuses, shocks good manners. For this reason, after the first or second request, it is allowable to put the hat on, unless one is in some province or kingdom where the usage is otherwise. In fact, amongst equals, or with the aged, or those who belong to religious orders, or with domestics, it is allowable to grant that request to one's equal or to a younger man at the very first time. However, those of equal rank and those of minor differences in rank usually make the request and put on their hats at the same time. All of these remarks on polite conduct must also be extended to the order to be observed in taking places and in sitting down; for the pleasure taken in ceremonies and compliments is really irksome.

28th: If anyone comes to speak to you while you are sitting, stand up although he be your inferiour. And when you present seats, let it be to every one according to his degree.

Si vous estes assis, lors que quelq'un vous vient rendre visite, leuez-vous dés qu'il approche, si la dignité de la personne demande cette déférence comme s'il à quelque advantage sur vous, s'il vous est égal, ou inferieur; mais non pas fort familier. Si vous vous reposez chez vous, ayãt quelque siège, faites en soite de traiter chacun selon son merite. [Maxims, III-5]

If you are sitting down when anyone pays you a call, rise as soon as he comes near, whether his position demands that deference (having precedence over you), or if he be your equal, or inferior; but not if you are on very intimate terms. If you are in your own house, having any seat to offer, manage to treat each guest according to his station.

29th:   When you meet with one of greater quality than yourself, stop and retire, especially if it be at a door or any straight place, to give way for him to pass.

Quand vous recontrez dés personnes à qui vous devez du respect, outre les devoirs d'une salutation ordinaire, vous estes obligé de vous arrester quelque peu de temps, ou de rebrousser chemin jusqu'à l'entrée des portes, ou aux coins des ruës, pour leur donner passage. [Maxims, III-6]

In meeting those to whom you should show respect, beyond the salutations which are their due, you should stop a little or retreat to a threshold, or to the corner of the street so as to make way for them.

Rules of Civility

Walker says: "If you meet a superior in a narrow way, stop and press to make him more room."

30th: In walking, the highest place in most countries seems to be on the right hand. Therefore, place yourself on the left of him whom you desire to honour; but if three walk together the middle place is the most honourable. The wall is usually given to the most worthy if two walk together.

S'il arrive que vous faciez la promenade avec eux, vous leur laisserez toûjours la place hōnorable, qui est celle qui sera marquée par l'usage. À parler generalmént, il semble que plusieurs Nations ont passé en coustume que la droite soit tenuë pour une marque de reverence, de telle sorte, que quand quelq'un veut deferer à un autre, il le mette à sa droite, en prenant sa gauche. Lors que trois hōmes se promenent ensemble, le plus qualifié a toûjours le milieu; celuy qui tient la droite, a le second lieu, & l'autre qui reste à la gauche, n'a que le troisiéme. Mais en France, quand l'on se promene au long d'un mur, par ce que ce lieu est presque toûjours plus elevé & plus net à cause de sa pente, la coûtume porte presque par tout qu'elle soit laisséе au plus qualifié, & particuliérement quand deux personnes marchēt ensemble. [Maxims, III-7]

If you happen to take a walk, always give your superiors the place of honour, which is that pointed out by usage. Generally speaking, it appears that several

nations have made it a custom that the right should always be held as a mark of esteem, so that, when anyone wishes to honour another, then one puts him on the right, himself taking the left. When three walk together, he of the highest rank always has the middle; he who has the second rank takes the right, and the third who remains has the left. When in France, and walking by the side of a wall, that place being almost always higher and cleaner because of the slope, the custom is that it be yielded to the man of the highest quality, particularly when two are walking together.

31st: If any one person far surpasses others, either in age, estate, or merit, yet would give his place to one meaner than himself, whether in his own house or elsewhere, the lesser one ought not to accept it. So as not to appear uncivil, the superior ought not to offer it [the preference or place of honor] above once or twice.

Si celuy qui se trouvera beaucoup plus avancé en âge, ou avantagé en dignité, soit en sa maison ou en quelqu' autre lieu, veut honorer son inferieur, comme il n'est pas à propos que cet inferieur s'en estime digne, de mesme aussi ne faut-il pas que celuy qui est superieur, l'en presse avec trop de soin, ou luy témoigne sa déférence plus d'une ou deux

George Washington's

fois, de crainte que l'assiduité de sa supplication reïterée ne rabatte quelque chose de la bõne opinion que celuy qui le refuse, avoit cõceu de son addresse & de sa courtoisie, ou qu'il luy fasse commettre enfin une incivilité. [Maxims, III-9]

If he who is much the older, or has the advantage of rank wishes, in his house or elsewhere, to honour his inferior, as it is not fitting that such inferior should think himself worthy, so also the superior must not press him too much or show such deference more than once or twice, lest the urgency of his reiterated requests lower somewhat the good opinion which he who refuses had conceived of his tact and courtesy, or lest, ultimately, it cause him to be guilty of some incivility.

32[d]:   To one that is your equal, or not much inferiour, you are to give the chief place in your lodging. And he to whom it is offered ought, at the first to refuse, but at the second offer to accept, though not without acknowledging his own unworthiness.

Mais entre les égaux, il est bien à propos en recevant quelqu'un dans sa maison, de luy donner la place la plus honnorable. Et celuy à qui l'on fait un si bon accueil, en doit faire quelque refus d'abord, mais à la seconde instance de son amy, il luy doit obeyr. [Maxims, III-10]

But amongst equals, it is quite right, in receiving anyone into one's house, to give him the most honorable place. The person to whom one accords such a good reception ought at first rather to refuse it but, when his friend insists a second time, he ought to obey him.

33[d]:   They that are in dignity or in office have, in all places, precedency; but whilst they are young they ought to respect those that are their equals in birth or other qualities, even though they have no public charge.

À ceux qui ont le cõmandement, & qui sont dans le pouvoir, ou qui exercent les Charges de Judicature, l'on donne toûjours les premiè res places en toute sorte de compagnie. Mais qu'ils sçachent eux-mesmes que s'ils sont jeunes, ils sont obligez de respecter ceux qui sont d'aussi noble maison qu'eux, ou qui les devãcent de beaucoup en âge, & sont honorez du degré de Doctorat; quoy qu'ils n'exercent aucune charge publique. Et bien plus, ils leur doivent d'abord remettre la premier place qu'il leur avoient deferé, & en suitte avec modestie, recevoir c'est honneur comme une grâce.
[Maxims, III-12]

PRESIDENT.—1789.

In every company, the first position is always given to those in command, those in power, or who exercise judicial charge. But if they are young, they should realize that they should respect other members of the

houses as noble as their own, or who are much older,
and those honored with the degree of Doctor though
not exercising any public function. Moreover, at first
they ought to return an offer of the highest place, and
afterwards receive that honour modestly, as a favour.

34th: It is good manners to prefer them
         to whom we speak before ourselves,
         especially if they be above us - with
         whom in no sort we ought to begin.

Il est de la derniere civilité de parler toûjours
mieux de ceux avec qui nous avons à converser, que
de vous mesmes. Et particuliérement quand ce sont
des personnes élevées audessus de nous, avec qui il
ne faut iamais contester en aucune maniere.
[Maxims, III-13]

It is the height of politeness always to speak better
of those with whom we converse than of ourselves.
And particularly when they are persons of a superior
rank to ourselves, with whom we ought never to dispute
in any fashion.

In 1552, Giovanni della Casa notes with sadness
that too many are "so infatuated with themselves that
they overlook other people." [*Galateo*, Chap. 18]
Della Casa endorses numerous distinctions in
social rank, but Conway does not find the second
clause of Rule #34 in the original French Maxims.

35th: Let your discourse with men of
          business be short and comprehensive.

Le temps & le lieu, l'âge & la difference des
personnes doivent regler tout cét usage de
compliments qui se fait parmy les plus polis, &
particuliérement ceux qui consistent dans les paroles.
Mais l'on doit tracher court avec les personnes
affairées & ne leur presenter plus aux nez toutes ses
agreables fleurettes; il le faut épargner, & se faire
entendre plustost par mines, qu'avec des paroles.
[Maxims, III-15]

Time and place, age and differences between
persons, ought to regulate the whole custom of
compliments as is performed amongst the most polite,
especially compliments that consist of words. But one
should cut matters short with men of business, and not
put one's fine flowerets under their nose. One should
spare them and make himself understood rather by
looks than by words.

36th: Artificers and persons of low degree
          ought not to use many ceremonies to
          Lords, or others of high degree, but
          respect and highly honour them.
          Those of high degree ought to treat
          their lessers with affability and
          courtesy, without arrogancy.

Comme le soin de la civilité la plus raffinée ne doit pas beaucoup travailler les esprits des Artisants & de la lie du peuple, enuers les Grands & les Magistrats; aussi est-il raisonnable qu'ils ayent soin de leur rendre de l'honneur. De mesme il est à propos que la Nobelesse les traitte doucement & les épargne, & qu'elle évite toute sorte de superbe. [Maxims, III-16]

Care for the most refined politeness should not be much trouble on the minds of artisans and of the dregs of the people, as regards Nobles and Magistrates; while it is reasonable that they should take care to honour their betters, so it is also right that the nobility should treat their lessers gently, and spare them, and avoid all manner of arrogance.

37th: In speaking to men of quality, do not lean, nor look them full in the face, nor approach too near them. At least, keep a full pace from them.

En parlant aux personnes qualifiées, ne vous appuyez point de corps; ne levez poinct vos yeux jusques sur leur visage; ne vous en approchez pas trop prés, & faites en sorte que ce ne soit iamais qu'à un grand pas de distãce. [Maxims, III-18]

In speaking to persons of quality, do not lean your body on anything; do not raise your eyes to their face;

George Washington's

do not go too near them, and manage to keep a full step in distance.

DEATH.—1799.

38th: In visiting the sick, do not presently play the physician if you be not knowing therein.

Quand vous visiterez quelque malade, ne faites pas aussi-tost le Medicin, si vous n'estes point experimenté en cette science. [Maxims, III-19]

When you go to see any sick person, do not immediately act the physician if you are not experienced in that science.

39th: In writing or speaking, give to every person his due title, according to his degree and the custom of the place.

Lors que vous addresserez des lettres à des personnes qui seront dans l'estime publique; vous vous gouvernerez auprès d'eux, selon la coustume du pays & le degré de leur dignité. Quand vous aurez achevé vos lettres, rélisez-les, pour en oster les fautes; mettez de la poudre sur l'éscriture, lors qu'il en sera besoin & ne pliez iamais vostre papier que les characteres ne soient bien deschez, de crainte qu'ils ne s'effacent. [Maxims, III-20]

In addressing letters to persons who are held in public esteem, you will be regulated by the customs of the country and the degree of the persons' dignity. When you have finished your letters, and read them over again so as to correct mistakes; sand the writing, and never fold your paper until the letters are quite dry, lest they be effaced.

40th: Strive not with your superiors in argument, but always submit your judgment to others with modesty.

Strive not with thy superiors, in argument or discourse, but always submit thy opinion to their riper judgment, with modesty (since the possibility of erring doth rather accompany green more than gray hairs). [Hawkins, II-20]

SURVEYOR, 1748.

41st: Undertake not to teach your equal in the art that he himself professes; it flavours of arrogancy.

Do not undertake to teach thy equal in the art himself professeth, for that will savour of arrogancy and serve for little other than to brand thy judgment with rashness. [Hawkins, II-21]

According to Moncure Conway, the original French Maxims do not contain any language that resembles George Washington's Rule #41.

Obadiah Walker, Master at University College, Oxford, gives us an interesting academic observation:
"Cautious also must be he who discourseth, even of that he understands, amongst persons of that profession. An affectation that more scholars than wise men are guilty of, I mean, [is] to discourse with every man in his own faculty, except it be by asking questions and seeming to learn."

42ᵈ: Let your ceremonies in courtesy be proper to the dignity of the place of the person with whom you converse. It is absurd to act ye the same with a clown and a Prince.

Let thy ceremonies in courtesy be proper to the dignity and place of him with whom thou conversest. For it is absurd to honour a clown with words courtly and of magnificence. [Hawkins, II-22]

"LET YOUR CEREMONIES IN COURTESY
BE PROPER ..."

43^d: Do not express joy before one who is
        sick or in pain, for that contrary
        passion will aggravate his misery.

Do not thou express joy before one sick, or in pain;
for that contrary passion will aggravate his misery. But
do thou rather sympathize [with] his infirmities, for
that will afford a grateful easement by a seeming
participation. [Hawkins, II-23]

Giovanni della Casa counsels that it is shameful
and unkind to mimick those who "stutter, or limp, or
are hunchbacked, or deformed." [*Galateo*, Chap. 19]

44th: When a man does all he can,
        though it succeeds not well,
        blame not he that did it.

Celuy qui fait tout ce qui luy est possible, pour
avancer vostre affaire, quoy qu'il ne la meine pas &
n'en puisse avoir le succez cōme vous l'esperez, ne
doit point entendre de reprimāde; puis qu'il est plus
digne de loüange que de blâme. [Maxims, IV-3]

The man who has done everything possible to
advance your affairs, even though his efforts were
imperfect and may not bring the success you had
hoped for, should not be showered with reprimands;
since he is more worthy of praise than of blame.

45th: Being to advise or reprehend anyone, consider whether it ought to be public or in private, presently or at some other time, in what terms to do it and, in reproving, show no signs of choler but do it with all sweetness and mildness.

Si vous avez à exhorter ou reprendre quelqu'un, prenez bien garde, s'il est plus à propos de le faire en particulier ou en public, en ce temps ou en un autre, bien plus, quelles paroles vous y devez employer. Et particuliérement lors que quelqu'un ayāt esté desia reprimādé d'autres fois, ne se corrige point des fautes passées, & ne promet point d'amandement. Et soit que vous donniez quelques avis, ou que vous fassiez quelque reprimande, donnez-vous de garde de vous mettre en cholere, au contraire pratiquez ces actions avec moderation & douceur. [Maxims, IV-4]

If you have to exhort or reproach anyone, consider whether it be better to do so in private or in public; at this time or another and, above all, what words you should use. And particularly when some one having been already reprimanded at other times does not correct himself of his past faults, and does not promise any amendment. And if you give any advice, or impart any reprimand, carefully avoid anger. On the contrary, do such acts with moderation and sweetness.

46th: Take all admonitions thankfully, in what time or place whatsoever given, but afterwards not being culpable, take a time or place convenient to let him know it that gave them.

Aussi quiconque se donnera la peine de vous remonstrer de quelque façõ, en quelque lieu, & en quelque temps qu'il le fasse, qu'il soit écouté de vostre part avec beaucoup de ressentiment de bienveillance & de reconnoissance. Et apres cela, si vous vous sentez innocent, & qu'il vous semble à propos de vous prouver tel, il vous sera bien permis de la faire; mais avec ce soin de prēdre bien vostre temps, & plustost pour luy en faire voir la verité, & le tirer de peine, & plus si vous estes en sa charge, ou si vous relevez de son pouvoir, que pour vous appuyer de quelque excuse. [Maxims, IV-5]

Also when anyone takes the trouble to rebuke you, no matter how, where or when he does it, hear him, for your part, with much feeling of goodwill and acknowledgment. And after that, if innocent and it seems right to prove yourself so, you will be quite at liberty to do so; being careful however, to choose a proper time, and rather to make him see the truth and relieve him from anxiety - the more if you are in his charge or depend on his authority - than to defend yourself with some excuse.

47th: Mock not, nor jest at anything of importance. Break no jests that are sharp and biting, and if you deliver anything witty and pleasant, abstain from laughing thereat yourself.

Ne vous amusez point aux equivoques ny en matiere importante, ny en choses honteuses. Si vous trouvez bon de railler, gardez vous bien de mordre, & bien plus de déchirer comme un chien. Que les bons-mots & les rencontres soient tirées du suient, que les uns & les autres ayent leur gentillesse & leur pointe, sans attirer l'indignation de personne. Que les plaisâteries ne soient point comme celles des bouffons, qui font rire par des représentations extravagâtes, & des actions déshonnestes. Si vous rencontrez joliment, si vous donnez quelque bon-mot, en faisant rire les autres, empêschez-vous-en, le plus qu'il vous sera possible. [Maxims, IV-7]

Do not divert yourself with double-entendres, neither in important nor in mean matters. If you find good occasion for a joke, be careful not to bite, still less to tear, like a dog. Witticisms and repartee should be to the point, and have refinement and appropriateness without exciting the indignation of any. Do not let your pleasantries degenerate into that of buffoons, who raise laughter by extravagant representations and indecent actions. And if you are clever in repartee, if you say a good thing, manage if possible, in making others laugh, to abstain from it yourself.

48th: Wherein you reprove another, be
unblameful yourself. For example
is more prevalent than precepts.

*Be sure thy conversation be in that point virtuous,
wherein thou art desirous to retaine another, least thy
actions render thy advice unprofitable, since the
ratification of any advice is the serious prosecution of
that virtue. For example hath ever been more
prevalent than precept.* [Hawkins, III-8]

In 1552, Giovanni della Casa asserts that "things
are more easily said than done ... It is not enough to
know the theory and the rules, it is also necessary ...
to put them into effect." [*Galateo*, Chap. 25]

49th: Use no reproachful language against
anyone, neither curse nor revile.

*Use no reproachful language against any man, nor
curse or revile. For improperations and imprecations
will rather betray thy affections than in any manner
hurt him against whom thou utters them.*
[Hawkins, III-11]

50th: Be not hasty to believe flying reports
to the disparagement of any.

George Washington's

Thou oughtest not, too suddenly, to believe a flying rumor of a friend or any other. But let charity guide thy judgment until more certainty. For by this means thou securest his reputation and frees thy self of rashness. [Hawkins, III-10]

51st: Wear not your clothes foul, ripped or dusty, but see to it that they be brushed once every day at least; and take heed that you approach not to any uncleanness.

Que vos habits ne demeurent point sales, déchirez, couverts de poussiere, ou pelez. Qu'ils soient tous les jours du moins une fois nettoyez avec les époussettes. Et prenez bien garde aussi en quel lieu vous assoirez, où vous vous mettrez à genoux, où vous vous accouderez, que le lieu ne soit point mal propre, ny rēply d'immondices. Ne portez point le manteau sur le bras, à l'imitation des Fanfarons. Et menttant bas ou vostre robbe, ou vôtre māteau, pliez les bien proprement & adroitement, & prenez bien garde où vous les posez. [Maxims, V-4]

Do not let your clothes be dirty, torn, covered with dust or threadbare. Have them brushed at least once a day. And take care also where you sit down or kneel, or rest your elbows, that it be not unfit or filthy. Do not carry your cloak over your arm in the style of the swaggerers. When you take off your coat, or your cloak, fold them properly and carefully, and then take care as to where you put them down.

52^d: In your apparel, be modest and endeavour to accommodate nature rather than to procure admiration. Keep to the fashion of your equals, such as are civil and orderly, with respect to times and places.

Choisissez toûjours des habits semblables à ceux de vos compagnons qui passent pour les plus honnestes & moderez, en considerant les lieux & les temps avec discretion. Et outre cela, faites qu'en ce poinct vous paroissiez souhaitter d'estre vestu le plus simplement & modestement de tous vos égaux, bien plustost que d'affecter les plus beaux vestements. [Maxims, V-5]

Always choose clothing similar to those, among your company, who are known for their propriety and moderation in the discreet consideration of the time and place. Make it a point to appear in your dress as the most simple and modest of all your equals, rather than to affect the most extravagant clothing.

Conway attributes the "accommodate nature" phrase to Hawkins; but, curiously, the Hawkins text [Hawkins IV-6] lacks any reference for dressing in

the fashion of ones equals, or selecting clothing that
would be appropriate for a particular time or place.

53[d]:   Run not in the streets, neither go
          too slowly, nor with your mouth
          open. Go not shaking your arms,
          nor stamping nor throwing your feet
          about. Walk not upon your toes,
          nor in a dancing, skipping manner;
          walk not in a stoop.

Faites en sorte quand vous marchez, de ne pas
faire des démarches precipite´es, d'avoir la bouche
ouverte & comme beante; & de ne vous trop
demener le corps, ou le pancher, ou laisser vos
mains pendantes, ou remuer & secoüer les bras.
Sans frapper trop rudement la terre, ou letter à vos
pieds de part & d'autre. Cette sorte d'action
demande encore ces conditions: que l'on ne
s'arreste pas à retirer ses chausses en haut, dans le
chemin, que l'on ne marche sur les extremitez des
pieds, n'y en sautillant ou s'élevant, comme il se
pratique en la dance. Que l'on ne courbe point le
corps, que l'on ne baisse point la teste; que l'on
n'avance point à pas cõptez, que l'on ne se choque
point les talons l'un contre l'autre en entrant dans
l'Eglise, que l'on ne reste point teste nuë à la sortie,
si la devotion n'y oblige, comme lors qu'il est
question d'accompagner le Très-sainct Sacrement.
[Maxims, VI-1]

In walking, guard against hurried steps, or having your mouth open and gaping; and do not move your body too much, or stoop, or let your hands hang down, or move and shake your arms. Walk without striking the ground too hard or throwing your feet this way and that. Walking in public also requires these conditions: not to stop to pull up one's stockings in the street; not to walk on the toes, or in a skipping, rising way as in dancing. Do not stoop, nor bend the head; do not advance with measured steps; do not strike the heels against each other on entering church, nor leave it bareheaded, unless devotion requires it, as in accompanying the Holy Sacrament.

54th:   Play not the peacock, looking everywhere about you to see if you be well decked, if your shoes fit well, if your stockings sit neatly, and your clothes appear handsomely.

Ne vous amusez pas à vous quarer comme un Paon, & regarder superbement autour de vous, si vous estes bien mis, & bien chaussé, si vos hauts-déchausses & vos autres habits vous sons bienfaits. Ne sortez point de vostre chãbre, portant vostre plume à vostre bouche, ou sur vostre aureille. Ne vous amusez pas à mettre des fleurs à vos aureilles, à vostre bonnet, ou à vostre chappeau. Ne tenez point vostre mouchoir à la main, ou pendu à vostre

"PLAY NOT THE PEACOCK ..."

bouche, n'y à vostre ceinture, n'y sous vostre aiselle, n'y sur vostre espaule, ou caché sous vostre robbe. Mettez-le en lieu d'où il ne puisse être veu, & il puisse estre toutesfois cōmodément tiré, dez qu'il en sera besoin. Ne le presentez iamais à personne, s'il n'est tout blanc, ou presque pas deployé. [Maxims, VI-2]

Do not delight in strutting like a peacock, nor look proudly around to see if you are well decked, if your breeches and other clothes fit well. Do not leave your room carrying your pen in your mouth or behind your ear. Do not indulge yourself by putting flowers in your ears, cap or hat. Do not hold your pocket handkerchief in your hand, hanging from your mouth, at your girdle, under your armpit, on your shoulder, or stuffed under your coat. Put your handkerchief in some place where it cannot be seen, but from whence you may easily draw it when you want it. Never offer it to anybody unless it be quite clean, or hardly folded.

In 1552, Giovanni della Casa expresses his utter disdain for "some men who bend over at every step to pull up their stockings, and some who wiggle their behinds and strut like peacocks." [*Galateo*, Chap. 28]

55th: Eat not in the streets, nor in ye house, out of season.

Ne marchez iamais par les chemins, en mangeant, soit seul ou en compagnie, & particulièrement parmy la foule de la ville. Ne vous mettez pas mesme à manger en la maison hors de temps du repas, & du moins abstenez vous en, quand il s'y rencontrera quelqu'un. [Maxims, VI-3]

Never walk on the roads while eating, whether alone or in company, especially amid the crowd in a town. Do not sit down to eat, even in your own house, out of the normal meal times; at least abstain from it in the presence of others.

56th: Associate yourself with men of good quality if you esteem your own reputation. For 'tis better to be alone than in bad company.

Et si vous voulez passer pour honneste, accostez vous toûjours des Gents-de-bien. Si vous n'en trouvez pas la commodité, ou par ce que vous n'en connoissez point, ou pour quelqu' autre raison, il vaut toûjours mieux que vous alliez seul, qu'en mauvaise compagnie. [Maxims, VI-5]

If you wish to be received as genteel, always go about with well-mannered people. If you cannot get the chance, from not knowing any, or any other reason, it is always better to go alone, than in bad company.

57th: In walking up and down in a house
with only one in company, if he be
greater than yourself, at the first give
him the right hand; and stop not until
he does; and be not the first that
turns, and when you do turn let it be
with your face towards him. If he be
a man of great quality, walk not with
him cheek by jowl but somewhat
behind him, but yet in such a manner
that he may easily speak to you.

Si vous promenez avec une personne seule dans
la maison, & qu'il soit d'une conditiō qui luy fasse
meriter quelque déférence, dès le premier pas de la
promenade, ne manquez pas de luy donner la droite.
Ne cessez point de marcher, s'il ne vient à s'arrester.
Ne changez pas le premier le divertissement, & en
vous tournant, ne luy montrez iamais les épaules;
mais toûjours le visage. Si elle est dans une charge
relevée, gardez bien de marcher d'un pas tout à fait
égal; mais suivez tant soit peu derriere, avec tant de
justesse pourtant & de moderatiō, qu'elle vous
puisse bien parler sans s'incōmoder. Si elle vous est
égale allez d'un mesme pas tout le long de la
promenade, & ne tournez pas toûjours le premier, à
chaque bout de champ; ne faites pas si souvent des
pauses au milieu du chemin sans suiet. Car cette
liberté ressent sa grandeur & donne du
mécontentement. Celuy qui tient le milieu dans une

George Washington's

compagnie dont il est environné, si ceux qui la composent, sont égaux, ou presque égaux, il se doit tourner une fois à droit dans la promenade, & s'ils se rencontrent notablement ineaux, il se doit plus souvent tourner vers le plus qualifié. Enfin que ceux qui l'environment, viennent toûjours à se détourner de son costé & en mesme temps que luy, non point devāt n'y apres; puis qu'il est comme le but de la promenade. [Maxims, VI-7]

If you are walking about the house alone with a person whose rank demands some deference, at the very first step be sure and give him the right hand. Do not stop walking if he does not wish to stop. Do not be the first to change the direction, and in turning never show him your shoulder but always your face. If he has a high public appointment, take care not to walk quite side by side with him but a very little behind him with so much exactness and moderation that he may be able to speak to you without inconvenience. If he is your equal in rank, keep step with him during the whole walk and do not always turn first at every end of the walk. Do not stop often midway without reason - such liberties touch upon his dignity and will give dissatisfaction. He who is the center of the company's attention should always to turn to the right once during the walk if others of the company are equal or nearly equal to him in rank; and if they are manifestly unequal, he should oftenest turn towards the most distinguished. Lastly, those who are about him should always turn round towards his side and at the same time as he, neither before nor after, as he is, so to speak, the object of the walk.

The repetition of the feminine gendered "elle" in Rule #57 is not an allusion to the female sex, but refers to the earlier "une personne," despite uses of "qu'il" and "s'il." Conway reports that he finds no allusions to the female sex in the original Maxims.

58th: Let your conversation be without malice or envy, for 'tis a sign of a tractable and commendable nature. And in all causes of passion admit reason to govern.

Let thy conversation be without malice or envy, for that is a sign of a tractable and commendable nature. And in all causes of passion, admit reason for thy governess. So shall thy reputation be either altogether inviolable, or at the least not stained with common tinctures. [Hawkins, V-9]

59th: Never express anything unbecoming, nor act against ye Rules moral in front of your inferiours.

Never express anything unbeseeming, nor act against the Rules moral, before thy inferiours. For in these things, thy own guilt will multiply crimes by example and, as it were, confirm ill by authority. [Hawkins, V-10]

As Obadiah Walker put it: "A man should not divertise himself with his inferiors, nor make his servants privy to his infirmities and failures."

60th: Be not immodest, in urging your friends to discover their secrets.

Be not immodest in urging thy friend to discover his secrets, lest an accidental discovery of them work a breach in your amity. [Hawkins, V-11]

61st: Utter not base or frivolous things amongst grave and learned men; nor very difficult questions or subjects, nor things hard to be believed, among the ignorant. Stuff not your discourse with sentences when you are amongst your betters or your equals.

Dans la conversation de Gents doctes & habiles ne debitez pas des bagatelles; et n'avancez pas des discours trop réleves parmy les ignorants, qu'ils ne soient point capables d'éntendre, ou qu'ils ne puissent pas croire fort facilement. Ne débutez pas toûjours par des proverbes, particulie´rement parmy vou égaux, & bien moins avec vos superieurs ... [Maxims, VII-1]

*When talking with learned and clever men, do not
introduce trifles; and do not bring forward too
advanced conversation before ignorant people, which
they cannot understand or easily believe. Do not
always begin with proverbs, especially among your
equals, and still less with your superiors ...*

Hawkins had used the French word "farce,"
instead of the "stuff" of the Washington MS. Farce
was generally understood to mean alternately, either
"a dramatic representation stuffed with ludicrous
conceits," or "a swelling out or extending of, and
filling with mingled ingredients."

62ᵈ: Speak not of doleful things in a time
of mirth, or at the table. Speak not of
melancholy things such as death and
wounds, and if others mention them,
change the discourse if you can.
Tell not your dreams, but to your
intimate friends.

... Ne parlez point de choses à contre-temps, ou
qui puissent choquer les espirits de vos Auditeurs.
Parmy les banquets & dans les jours de rejoüissance
ne mettez point sur le tapis de tristes nouvelles,
point de récits de rudes calamitez, point d'ordures,
point de déshonnesteté, point d'afflictions. Bien au

contraire si tels discours se trouvent entamez par quelqu' autre, faites vostre possible pour en détourner adroitement la suitte. Ne contez iamais vos songes qu'à de vos confidents, & encore que ce soit pour profiter de leur interpretation; vous gardant bien d'y donner aucune croyance.
[Maxims, VII-1]

... Do not speak of things out of place, or of such as may shock your hearers. At banquets and on days of rejoicing do not bring up sorrowful news or accounts of sad calamities, nor filth, nor indecencies, nor afflictions. On the contrary, if such conversation is begun by someone else, do your best to adroitly turn the subject. Never share your dreams with anyone but your confidants, and then only to profit by their interpretations; taking good care not to put the least belief in it.

Ever the incisive wordsmith, Walker counseled: "nor tell your dreams when perhaps your best waking actions are not worth the reciting."

63[d]:   A man ought not to value himself of his achievements or rare qualities, his riches, his titles, his virtue or his kindred; but he need not speak meanly of himself, either.

Une personne bien nourrie ne s'amuse iamais à
faire parade de ses belles actions, du son esprit, de
sa vertu, & de ses autres bonnes & loüables qualités,
au contraire il ne faut iamais s'entretenir avec les
autres de sa haute naissance, ou de ses grandeurs, si
l'on n'y est contrainct. Il ne faut pas aussi se ravaller
entièrment. [Maxims, VII-2]

A well-bred person never makes a parade of his
good actions, his wit, virtue and other praiseworthy
qualities. On the contrary, one should never speak
with another about his high birth, the nobility of his
parents, or his wealth or dignities, unless obliged to do
so. But one need not efface himself altogether.

64th: Break not a jest where none take
pleasure in mirth. Laugh not aloud,
nor at all without occasion.
Deride no man's misfortune, although
there may seem to be some cause.

Il ne faut pas se mettre sur la raillerie, quand il
n'est point temps de solastrer. Gardez-vous bien
d'éclater en risées, d'y passer les bornes de la bien-
séance, & de le faire sans un sulet raisonnable, pour
suivre l'inclinatiõ qui vous porte à rire. Ne prenez
iamais sujet de rire du malheur d'autruy, quoy qu'il
semble en quelque façõ digne de risée.
[Maxims, VII-3]

*Jesting must be avoided when it is out of season.
Take care to keep from bursting out into laughter
beyond the limits of good manners, and of doing so
without reasonable cause, merely from an inclination
to laugh. Never laugh at the misfortunes of others,
although they seem in some sort laughable.*

65th: Speak not injurious words, neither
in jest nor earnest. Scoff at no one,
although they give occasion.

Ne donnez iamais de sobriquet, soit dans le jeu,
pou bien hors du jeu. Gardez-vous bien de picquer
qui que ce puisse estre; ne vous mocquez d'aucune
personne, particulierement d'entre celles qui sont
qualifées, quoy qu'avec occasion. [Maxims, VII-4]

*Never give nicknames, whether in fun or not. Take
care not to hurt anybody, whoever it may be; do not
mock anyone, especially persons of distinction,
although there may be occasion.*

66th: Be not froward [irritable], but friendly
and courteous. Be the first to salute,
to hear, and to answer; and be not
pensive when it's a time to converse.

Ne vous rendez point morne & de fâcheux
abord, mais affable & prompt à rendre de bons
offices; & soyez toûjours le premier à saluër.
Entendez bien ce que l'on vous dit & y respondez.
Ne vous rétirez point à l'écart, quand le devoir vous
engage à la conversation. [Maxims, VII-5]

Do not be glum and unfriendly in your approach,
but affable and prompt in rendering kind offices; and
always be the first to salute. Listen carefully to what
is said and respond. Do not keep aloof when duty
requires that you take part in a conversation.

67th: Detract not from others; neither be excessive in commending them.

Gardez-vous bien de médire d'aucune personne
ou de vous entretenir des affaires d'autruy. Et
mesme souvenez vous de garder la moderation
dans vos loüanges. [Maxims, VII-6]

Take care not to speak ill of anyone or to gossip of
other people's affairs. At the same time do not forget
moderation in your praises.

Mt. Vernon and Brookhiser mistakenly follow
Dr. Toner, inserting "commanding" as the last word
of Rule #67. Conway's correction is reiterated here.
Turning the phrase a bit, Obadiah Walker puts it:
"Carry even between adulation and sourness."

68th: Go not thither, where you know not whether you shall be welcome or not. Give not advice without being asked and, when desired, do it briefly.

Ne vous ingérez pas dans les entretiens & les consultations, où vous ne serez pas asseuré d'estre que l'on ne vous l'ait demandé, si toutesfois vous n'estes le premier en authorité, & que ce ne soit point à contre-temps, ou sans apparence de quelque avantage. Quand vous en estes prié, abrégez vostre discours, & prenez de bonne heure le noeud de l'affaire à démesler. [Maxims, VII-7]

Do not force yourself into interviews or consultations at which you are not sure of being welcome, and unless you happen to be the highest in authority, never give your advice when it has not been asked, and do not let it be seen as out of place or without prospect of any benefit. When your opinion is requested, be brief and reach quickly the knot of the matter under discussion.

69th: If two contend together, take not the part of either unconstrained; and be not obstinate in your opinion. In things to which you are indifferent, be a part of the major side.

Si deux personnes ont quelque chose à decider ensemble, ne prenez le party n'y de l'un, n'y de l'autre, si quelque grande raison ne vous y oblige. Ne soustenez pas vos sentiments avec une trop grande obstination. Dans les matières où les opiniõs sont libres, prenez toûjours le party qui est le plus appuyé. [Maxims, VII-8]

If two persons have anything to decide between themselves, do not take the part of either unless some greater reason obliges you to do so. Do not maintain your ideas too obstinately. In matters in which opinions are freely given, always take the side which has the most support.

Walker suggested: "Thrust not yourself to be moderator or umpire in controversies, 'til required."

70th: Reprehend not the imperfections of others - for that belongs to [meaning, is the province of] parents, masters and superiors.

Ne faites pas le censeur & le juge des fautes d'autruy, car cela n'apparient qu'aux maistres, aux pères, & à ceux qui ont quelque superiorité. Il vous est toutesfois permis de faire paraître l'aversion que vous en cõcevez. Et vous pouvez bien quelquesfois donner avis avantageux au défaillants.
[Maxims, VII-9]

Do not be the censor and judge of other peoples' faults, for that only belongs to masters, fathers and those who have some superiority. But it is nevertheless allowable for you to show an aversion you have conceived. And at times you may give advantageous advice to those who are in the wrong.

71st: Gaze not at the marks or blemishes of
         others, and ask not how they came.
         What you may speak in secret to your
         friend, deliver not before others.

Ne vous amusez pas à considerer curieusement
les défauts ou les taches, quoy que naturelles,
particuliérement si elles se rencontrent au visage; &
ne vous enquerez pas d'où elles ont procedé. Ce
que vous diriez bien volontiers en l'oreille à un amy,
doit estre conservé sous la clef du silèce, lors que
vous trouvez en compagnie. [Maxims, VII-10]

Do not take pleasure in curiously examining defects
or blemishes, although natural, especially if they be in
the face; nor inquire about what their cause. What
one would readily say in the ear of a friend should be
preserved under the key of silence when in society.

72^d: Speak not in an unknown tongue in
         company, but in your own language
         and that as those of quality do,
         and not as the vulgar would.
         Sublime matters treat seriously.

Ne vous seruez iamais en vos discours &
n'employez une langue qui ne vous est pas bien
cognuë & familière, si ce n'est en une occasiõ bien
présante, pour donner plus clairement à connoistre

vostre pensée. Parlez toûjours en la vostre
maternelle & natale, non pas grossierement, comme
la lie du peuple, ou les pauvres cham-brieres; mais
comme les plus délicats & les plus gros Bourgeois,
avec érudition & avec élégance. Et prenez à tâche
d'observer en vos discours les regles de l'honnesteté
& de la modestie; & vous gardez bien de ces contes
un peu trop libres; ne les faites n'y en l'oreille d'un
autre, n'y ne les poussez par jeu avec profusiõ.
N'employez point de termes bas & ravalez ou
populaires en des matières hautes & reluées.
[Maxims, VII-11]

*In your conversation, never use a language with
which you are not thoroughly acquainted and familiar
unless, in some very urgent case, to render your idea
more clearly. Always speak in your mother and native
tongue, not coarsely like the dregs of the people or poor
chamber-maids, but like the most refined and well-to-
do citizens with erudition and elegance. And in your
speech take care to observe the rules of decency and
modesty; be sure to avoid rather risky tales; do not
whisper tales to others, and do not indulge them too
frequently in sport. Do not use base or vulgar
expressions when the matter is serious and sublime.*

73[d]:   Think before you speak.
        Pronounce not imperfectly,
        nor bring out your words too hastily,
        but orderly and distinctly.

Ne vous mettez point à discourir, que vous ne vous y soyez bien preparé, & que vous n'ayez bien éstudié vostre sujet. Dans l'entretien ordinaire, n'allez point chercher de périphrases, point de subtilitez, n'y de figures. Ne confondez point vos paroles dans les coutumes d'une langue trop brusque & bégayante; mais aussi, ne parlez pas si lentement, & à tant de reprises, que vous donniez de l'ennuy. [Maxims, VII-12]

Do not begin speaking until you are quite prepared, and have studied your subject well. In ordinary conversation do not speak in periphrases, subtleties or figures of speech. Do not let your words become confused by an abrupt or hesitating delivery, and do not let your speech be so slow and broken as to become tedious.

74th: When another speaks, be attentive yourself and disturb not the audience. If any hesitate in his words, help him not, nor prompt him without it being desired; interrupt him not, nor answer him until his speéch be ended.

Quand quelqu' autre parle, prenez garde de donner sujet à ses Auditeurs de s'n detourner; & pour vous, écoutez-le favorablement & avec attention, sans déstourner les yeux d'un autre costé, ou vous arrester à quelqu' autre pensée. Si quelqu'un a de la peine à tirer ses mots comme par force, ne vous amusez pas à luy en suggérer, pour faire paraître quelque désir d'aider celuy qui parle, si'l ne vient à vous en prier, ou que le tout se passe dans le particulier, & qu'encore cette personne soit de vos plus intimes & familiers amis. Apres tout ne l'interrompez point, & ne luy répliquez en aucune maniere, jusques à ce que luy-mesme ait achevé. [Maxims, VII-13]

When another person is speaking, take precaution not to draw off the attention of his listeners; and as for yourself, listen to him favourably and attentively, without turning your eyes aside or directing your thoughts elsewhere. If anyone finds difficulty in searching for the right word, do not amuse yourself by suggesting words to him, so as to show a desire to assist the speaker, unless he invites you or you are quite in private and the speaker is one of your most intimate and familiar friends. Above all, do not interrupt him, and reply to him in no way until he has finished.

The anonymous French version of this Rule was: "It is not civil when a person of quality hesitates or stops in his discourse for you to strike in, though with pretense of helping his memory." Hawkins put it a little differently: "If any drawl forth his words, help him not." Drawl was then understood to mean "a protracted modulation of the voice."

75th: In the midst of discourse, ask not what is being treated; but if you perceive any stop because of your arrival, politely ask the speaker to proceed. If a person of quality comes in while you converse, it is handsome to repeat what was said before.

Quand vous arrivez sur la moitié de quelque discours, ne vous enquerez pas du sujet de l'entretien - car cela est trop hardy & ressent l'hōme d'authorité. Suppliez plûtost honnestement & courtoisement que l'on le poursuive, si vous voyez qu'il se soit interrompu à vostre arrivée, parquel que sorte de déférence. Au contraire s'il suruient quelqu'un, lors que vous parlerez & particuliérement si c'est une personne qualifée & de mérite, il est de la bien-séance de faire une petite recapitulation de ce qui a esté avancé, & de poursuivre la déduction de tout le reste de la matière. [Maxims, VII-14]

If you arrive in the middle of any discussion, do not ask what it is about - for that is too bold and savors of one in authority. For the sake of politeness, ask genteelly and courteously that the conversation be continued, if you see that the speaker has paused upon your arrival. On the other hand, if anyone comes in while you are speaking, and particularly if it is a person of quality or merit, it is in accordance with good manners to give a small recapitulation of what has been advanced and then proceed to complete the discussion of the balance of the matter.

George Washington's

76th: While you are talking, point not
with your finger at him with whom
you discourse, nor approach
too near him to whom you talk,
especially to his face.

Ne mõtrez point au doigt la personne dont vous parlez, & ne vous approchez point trop près de celuy que vous entretenez, non plus que de son visage, à qui il faut toûjours porter quelque reverence. [Maxims, VI-17]

Do not point your finger at the person that you are speaking to, and do not go too near anyone with whom you are conversing, especially not near his face, which should always be held in some reverence.

77th: Treat with men at fit times about business, and whisper not in the company of others.

Si vous avez une affaire particulière à communiquer a l'une de deux personnes ou de plusieurs qui s'entretiennent ensemble, expédiez en trois mots, & ne luy dites pas en l'oreille ce que vous avez à proposer. Mais si la chose est secrette, tirez-la tant soit peu à l'écart, s'il vous est possible, & que rien ne vous en empesche; parlez luy en la langue que les assistants entendent. [Maxims, VI-18]

If you have any particular matter to communicate to one person among two or several persons who are talking together, finish it off in three words and do not whisper in his ear what you have to say. If the matter is a secret, take him a little to the side, if possible and nothing prevents it; speak to him in the language that is understood by those present.

78th:   Make no comparisons, and if any of the company be commended for any brave act of [sic - or] virtue, commend not another for the same.

Abstenez vous de faire des comparaisons des personnes l'une avec l'autre. Et partant si l'on donne des loüanges à quelqu'un pour une bonne action, ou pour sa vertu, gardez-vous bien de loüer la mesme vertu en quelqu' autre. Car toute comparaison se trouve odieuse. [Maxims, VII-21]

Abstain from drawing comparisons between different persons and, if anyone is praised for a good action, or for his virtue, do not praise another for the same. For all comparisons are odious.

Evidently, George Washington mistakenly wrote the "brave act of virtue" phrase into his MS version of the Rules. The distinction between virtuous and brave acts, made clear in older versions of the Rules, was somehow confused in translation. A substantial number of the Rules suggest that considerate and thoughtful restraint (rather than action) is often the appropriate course for a virtuous, civil person.

79th: Be not apt to relate news if you know
         not the truth thereof. In discoursing
         of things that you have heard, name
         not your author. Always, a secret
         discover not [that is, do not reveal].

Ne faites pas aisément dessein de rédire aux
autres les nouvelles & les rapports qui aurõt couru
touchant les rencontres des affaires, si vous n'avez un
garant de leur verité. Et ne vous amusez pas en
racontant ces vau-de-villes, d'en citer l'Autheur, que
vous ne soyez bien assueré qu'il ne le trouvera pas
mauvais. Gardez toûjours bien le secret qui vous a
esté confié & ne le ditez à personne, de crainte qu'il
ne soit divulgué. [Maxims, VII-22]

*Be not apt to relate rumors of events, if you know
not their truth. And in repeating such things, do not
mention your authority unless you are sure he will like
it. Always keep the secret confided to you. Tell it to
no one, lest it be divulged.*

In 1552, della Casa assures his readers that, "in
the long run, liars are neither believed nor listened
to ... their words are meaningless and their speech is
more or less empty air." [*Galateo*, Chap. 13]

According to Moncure Conway, the anonymous
French version of 1673 advises: "Discover not the
secret of a friend, it argues a shallow understanding
and a weakness."

80th: Be not tedious in discourse or in
         reading, unless you find the company
         to be pleased therewith.

Si vous racontez, ou lisez, ou entreprenez d'en
prouver par raisonnements quoy que ce soit,
tranchez-le-court, & particuliérement quand le sujet
en est peu importât, ou quad vous reconnoissez les
dégousts qu'en ont les Auditeurs. [Maxims, VII-23]

*If you are relating or reading anything, or arguing a
point, be brief; and particularly when the subject is of
little importance, or if you detect weariness in your
listeners.*

Della Casa suggests that anyone who expresses
their opinion with "much shyness" is subjecting their
listeners to "a slow death." [*Galateo*, Chap. 13]

81st: Be not curious to know the affairs
         of others; neither approach near to
         those that speak in private.

Ne témoignez pas de curiosité dans les affaires
d'autruy, & ne vous approchez de là où l'on parle en
secret. [Maxims, VII-24]

*Do not show any curiosity about the affairs of
other people, and do not go near the place where
people are talking in private.*

82ᵈ: Undertake not what you cannot
        perform. Be careful to keep your
        promises.

Ne vous chargez point d'une chose dont vous ne
vous pouvez acquiter; maintenez ce que vous avez
promis. [Maxims, VII-25]

Do not undertake anything that you cannot
complete; keep your promise.

83ᵈ: When you deliver a matter, do it
        without passion and with discretion,
        however mean ye person be that you
        deliver it to.

Quand vous faites une ambassade, un rapport,
ou donnez l'ouverture de quelque affaire, taschez de
le faire sans passion & avec discretion, soit que vous
ayez à traitter avec personnes de peu, ou personnes
de qualité. [Maxims, VII-27]

When you fulfill a mission, deliver a report, or
undertake the opening of any matter, try to do it
dispassionately and discreetly, whether those with
whom you have to treat are of humble origin or high
position.

84th: When your superiors talk to anybody, hearken [meaning attend, or listen eagerly] not thereto - and neither speak nor laugh.

Quand ceux qui ont sur vous commandement, parlent à quelqu'un, gardez-vous bien de parler, de rire ou de les éscouter. [Maxims, VII-27]

When your superiors talk to anyone, do not speak, laugh or listen.

85th: In the company of those of higher quality than yourself, speak not until you are asked a question. Then, stand upright, put off your hat, and answer in few words.

Estant avec de plus grands que vous principalement s'ils ont du pouvoir sur vous, ne parlez pas devāt que d'estre interrogé. Alors levez-vous debout, découvrez-vous, & répondez en peu de mots, si toutesfois l'on ne vous donne congé de vous asseoir, ou de vous tenir couvert. [Maxims, VII-30]

When you are with persons of higher station than yourself, and especially if they have authority over you, do not speak until you are interrogated. Then, rise, remove your hat, and answer in few words - unless indeed you are invited to remain seated, or to keep your hat on.

86th: In disputes, be not so desirous to overcome objections as not to give liberty to each one to deliver his opinion, and submit to ye judgment of ye major part, especially if they are judges of the dispute.

Dans les disputes qui arrivent, principalement en conversation, ne soyez pas si désireux de gagner, que vous ne laissiez dire à chacun son aduis, & soit que vous ayez tort, ou raison, vous deuez acquiescer au jugement du plus grand nombre, ou mesme des plus fascheux, & beaucoup plus de ceux de qui vous dépendez, ou qui sont juges de la dispute.
[Maxims, VII-31]

In disputes that arise, especially in conversation, do not be so desirous to overcome as not to leave each one the liberty to deliver his opinion; and regardless of whether you are right or wrong, you should acquiesce in the judgment of the majority, or even that of the most persistent, especially if they are your masters or patrons, or the judges of the disagreement.

87th:   Let your bearing be such as becomes
a man who is grave and settled,
and be attentive to what is said
in conversation. Contradict not
at every turn what others say.

Vostre maintien soit d'hōme moderé ment grave, posé & attentif a ce qui se dit, afin de n'avoir pas à dire à tout propos: "Comment ditez-vous? Comment se passe cela? Je ne vous ay pas entendu." Et d'autres semblables niaiseries. [Maxims, VII-35]

Let your bearing be that of a moderately grave, serious man, and be attentive to what is said so that you avoid having to say every moment: "What did you say? How did that happen? I did not understand you." And other similar foolish remarks.

Ne contredictes pas à tout bout de champ, à ce que disent les autres, en contestant & distant: "Il n'est pas ainsi, la chose est comme je la d'y ..." Mais rapportez-vous en à l'opinion des autres principalement dans les choses qui sont de peu de consequence. [Maxims, VII-33]

Do not continually contradict what others say, by disputing and saying: "That is not the case, it is as I say ..." Rather, defer to the opinion of others, especially in matters of little consequence.

88th: Be not tedious in discourse; make
not many digressions; nor repeat
often the same manner of discourse.

N'employez pas un an à vostre préface, & en
certaines longues excuses ou ceremonies, en disant,
"Monsieur, excusez-moy! Si je ne sçay pas si bien
dire, &c., toutsfois pour vous obeyr, &c. ...," &
autres semblables ennuyevses et sottes trainées de
paroles. Mais entrez promptement en matière tant
que faire se pourra avec une hardiesse moderée, et
puis poursuivez, sans vous troubler, jusqu' à la fin.
Ne soyez pas long; sans beaucoup de digressions;
ne reïterez pas souvent une mesme façõ de dire.
[Maxims, VII-39]

*Do not take a year in your preface, or in certain
long apologies or ceremonies, such as: "Pardon me Sir,
if I do not know how to express myself sufficiently well,
&c.; nevertheless in order to obey you, &c. ...," and
other similarly tedious and irritating circumlocutions.
But, enter promptly on the subject as far as possible,
with moderate boldness, then continue to the end
without hesitation. Do not be long-winded; avoid
digressions; do not repeat the same expression often.*

Giovanni della Casa counsels that well-mannered
men guard against speaking too much, "especially if
they know little," in order to "ease rather than
obstruct other people's wishes." [*Galateo*, Chap. 24]

"Do not take a year in your preface ..."

89th: Speak not evil of those who are absent, for it is unjust.

Speak not evil of one absent, for it is unjust to detract from the worth of any, or besmear a good name by condemning, where the party is not present to clear himself or undergo a rational conviction.
[Hawkins, VI-40]

90th: Being set at meat, scratch not, neither spit, cough nor blow your nose, except when there is a necessity for it.

Estant assis à table, ne vous grattez point, & vous gardez tant que vous pourrez, de cracher, de tousser, de vous moucher. Que s'il y a necessité, faites-le adroitement, sans beaucoup de bruit, en tournant le visage de costé. [Maxims, VIII-2]

Being seated at the table, do not scratch yourself, and if you can help it do not spit, cough or blow your nose. Should it be necessary, do so adroitly, with the least amount of noise, turning the face aside.

91st: Make no show of taking great delight in your victuals. Feed not with greediness. Cut your bread with a knife. Lean not on the table; neither find fault with what you have to eat.

Ne monstrez nullement d'avoir pris plaisir à la viande, ou au vin; mais si celuy que vous traittez, vous en demande vostre goust, vous pourrez luy respondre avec modestie & prudence. Beaucoup moins faut il blasmer les viandes, ou en demander 'autres, n'y davantage. [Maxims, VIII-8]

George Washington's

Do not make a show of taking delight in your food, or in the wine; but if your host asks you for your preference, you should answer with modesty and tact. Whatever you do, do not complain of the victuals, or ask for other dishes, or anything of that sort.

Ne prenez pas vostre repas en gourmand. [Maxims, VIII-3]

Do not eat like a glutton.

Ne rompez point le pain avec les mains, mais avec le cousteau, si ce n'éstoit un pain fort petil & tout frais, & que tous les autres fissent de mesme, ou la pluspart. [Maxims, VIII-4]

Do not break the bread with your hands but with a knife, unless, indeed, it is a small and quite fresh roll, and then, where the others present, or most of them, use their hands.

Ne vous jettez pas sur table, à bras estendus jusques aux coudes, & ne vous accostez pas indecemment les épaules ou les bras sur vostre siege. [Maxims, VIII-5]

Do not throw yourself on the table, as far as the elbows, and do not unbecomingly rest your shoulders or arms on your chair.

According to Conway it was a custom for George Washington to invite every guest at Mount Vernon to "call for" or select their wine of preference.

92ᵈ: Take no salt, nor cut bread,
         when your knife is greasy.

Prenant du sel, gardez que le cousteau ne soit gras. Quand il le faut nettoyer, ou la fourchette on le peut faire honnestement avec un peu de pain - ou comme il se pratique en certains lieux, avec la serviette - mais iamais sur le pain entier.
[Maxims, VIII-9]

In taking salt, be careful that the knife is not greasy. When necessary, your knife or fork may with propriety be cleaned on a piece of bread - or, as is done in some places, with the napkin - but it must never be wiped on the whole loaf.

93ᵈ: Entertaining anyone at table, it is
         decent to present him with meat.
         Undertake not to help others
         undesired by ye master or host.

Traittant quelqu'un, il est de la bien-séance de le servir en table, & luy presenter des viandes, voire mesme de celles qui sont proches de luy. Que si l'on estoit invité chez autruy, il est plus à propos d'attendre que le Maistre ou un autre serve, que de prendre des viandes soy-mesme, si ce n'estoit que le Maistre priast les conviez de prendre librement, ou que l'on fust en maison familiere. L'on se doit aussi peu ingerer à servir les autres hors de sa maison, où l'on avoir peu de pouvoir, n'étoit que le nombre des conviez fust grand, & que le Maistre de la maison ne peust pas avoir l'œil sur tout. Et pour lors l'on peut servir ceux qui sont proches de soy. [Maxims, VIII-10]

When entertaining anyone, it is good manners to serve him at table and to present the dishes to him, even such as are near him. When invited by another, it is more seemly to wait to be served by the host, or someone else, than to take the dishes oneself, unless the host begs the guests to help themselves freely or one is at home in the house. One should also avoid being officious in helping others when not in one's own house, where one has but little authority, unless the guests are very numerous and the host cannot attend to everything. In that case we may help those nearest us.

94th:   If you soak bread in the sauce, let it be no more than what you put in your mouth at one time; and blow not on your broth at the table, but stay until it cools of itself.

Si vous trempez en la saulce le pain ou la chair, ne les trempez pas derechef, apres y avoir mordu, trempez-y à chaque fois un morceau mediocre, qui se puisse manger tout d'une bouchée. [Maxims, VIII-14]

If you dip your bread or meat into the gravy, do not do so immediately after biting a piece off, but instead dip each time a moderately-sized morsel, which can be eaten at one mouthful.

Ne soufflez point sur les viandes. Mais si elles sont chaudes, attendez qu'elles se refroidissent. Le potage se pourra refroidir, le remuant modestement avec la cuillière, mais il ne sied pas bien de humer son potage en table, il le faut prendre avec la cuilliere. [Maxims, VIII-11]

Do not blow on the victuals, but if they are hot, wait until they cool. Soup may be cooled by stirring it gently with a spoon, but it is not becoming to drink up the soup at table. It should be taken with a spoon.

95th:   Put not your meat to your mouth with your knife in your hand; neither spit forth the stones of any fruit pie upon a dish, nor cast anything under the table.

Ne portez pas le morceau à la bouche, tenant le cousteau en la main, à la mode des villageois. [Maxims, VIII-17]

Do not carry a morsel to your mouth, with your knife in your hand, in the style of the uncouth.

Aussi ne semble-il bien séant de cracher les noyaux de prunes, cerises, ou autre chose semblable sur le plat ... Mais ... on doit les recueiller décemment, comme il à esté dit, en la main gauche, l'approchant à la bouche, & puis les metter sur le bord de l'assiette. [Maxims, VIII-16]

It is not good manners to spit out the kernels of prunes, cherries or anything of the kind on your plate ... but ... they should be decently collected from the mouth in the left hand and placed on the edge of the plate.

L'on ne doit point jetter sous la table, ou par terre, les os, les écorces, le vin ou autre chose semblable ...   [Maxims, VIII-15]

Bones, peel, wine and the like should not be thrown under the table ...

96th:   It is unbecoming to stoop much into one's meat. Keep your fingers clean and, when foul, wipe them on a corner of your table napkin.

Il set messeant de se baisser beau-coup sur son escuelle ou sur la viande. C'est assez de s'encliner un peu lors que l'on porte le morceau trempé à la bouche, de crainte de se salir, & puis redresser la teste. [Maxims, VIII-21]

*It is ill-bred to stoop too close to one's porringer or
to one's victuals. It suffices to bend a little when one
conveys a soaked morsel to one's mouth, in order to
avoid staining oneself, and then straighten up again.*

Ne vous nettoyez pas les mains à vostre pain.
S'il est entier, toutfois les ayant fort grasses, il
semble que vous les puissiez nettoyer premièrement
à un morceau de pain que vous ayez à manger tout
à l'heure & puis à la seruitte, afin de ne la point
tant salir. Ce qui vous arrivera rarement, si vous
sçauez vous servir de la cuillière, & de la fourchette,
selon le style des plus honnestes. Beaucoup moins
devez vous lêcher les doigts, principalement les
sucçant avec grand bruit. [Maxims, VIII-25]

*Do not clean your hands on a loaf. If your hands
are very greasy, you might partly clean them on a bit of
bread you are about to eat, then on your napkin, so as
not to soil the latter too much. This will rarely happen
if you know how to use both the spoon and fork in the
most genteel manner. You should not lick your fingers,
and certainly do not suck them with a loud noise.*

97th:   Put not another bit into your mouth
'till the former be swallowed. Let not
your morsels be too big for the jowls.

Ne portez pas le morceau à la bouche que l'autre ne soit avallé, & que tous soient tels qu'ils ne fassent pas enfler les jouës hors de mesure. Ne vous seruez pas des deux mains pour vous mettre le morceau à la bouche, mais seruez vous d'ordinaire de la droite. [Maxims, VIII-30]

Do not carry another morsel to your mouth until the previous one is swallowed, and let each morsel be such that the jaws will not stretch beyond measure. Do not use both hands to raise a morsel to the mouth but, usually, serve yourself with the right hand.

Our Florentine cleric, Giovanni della Casa, expresses his contempt for those who eat "like pigs with their snouts in the swill ... or rather gulp down their food with both their cheeks puffed out, as if they were blowing a trumpet." [*Galateo*, Chap. 5]

98th: Drink not, nor talk, with your mouth full. Neither gaze about you while you are drinking.

Ne boivez ayant le morcèau en la bouche; ne demandez point à boire, ne parlez, ne vous versez point à boire; & ne boivez cependant que vostre voisin boit, ou celuy qui est au haut bout. [Maxims, VIII-32]

Do not drink when your mouth is full of food; do not ask anything while drinking, nor talk, nor pour another drink; and do not drink just because your neighbor or the head of the table does.

En boivant, ne regardez point çà & là.
[Maxims, VIII-33]

While drinking, do not gaze about, here and there.

Conway tells us that the anonymous French writer of 1673 recommends that we keep our eyes "fixed at the bottom of the glass" while we drink.

99th: Drink not too leisurely, nor yet too hastily. Wipe your lips before and after drinking. Breath not when drinking, or ever, with too great a noise, for it is uncivil.

Ne boivez point trop lentement n'y trop à la haste, n'y comme en maschant le vin, n'y trop souvent n'y sans eau, car c'est à faire aux yurognes. Devāt & apres que vous aurez beu, effuyez-vous les lévres; & ne respirez pas avec trop grand bruit, n'y alors, n'y iamais, car c'est une chose bien incivile.
[Maxims, VIII-34]

Do not drink too slowly or too hastily, nor as if gulping the wine, nor too frequently, nor without water, as drunkards would do. Before and after drinking, wipe your lips; and do not make a loud breathing noise then, or any other time, for that is very impolite.

100th:   Cleanse not your teeth with the tablecloth, napkin, fork or knife; but if others do it, let it be done with a pick tooth [ie., toothpick].

Ne vous nettoyez pas les dents avec la nappe, ou la serviette, n'y avec le doigt, la fourchette, ou le cousteau. Ce seroit faire pis de le faire avec les ongles, mais faites-le avec le curedent. Aussi ne semble-il estre bien-séant de se les nettoyer en table, si ce n'éstoit que les auters le fissent, & que ce fust le coustume des mieux civilisez. [Maxims, VIII-36]

Do not clean your teeth with the tablecloth, or napkin, nor with your finger, fork or knife. It is still more objectionable to do so with the nails, rather, use a toothpick. Also, is does not appear well-bred to pick your teeth at the table unless others do so, and where such is a custom of the more refined.

As early as 1552, della Casa asserts that "it is not proper to rub one's teeth with one's napkin, and even less so with one's finger." [*Galateo*, Chap. 29]

101st: Rinse not your mouth in the presence
of others.

Ne vous rincez point la bouche avec du vin, pour
le reietter en presence des autres; mais sorty que
vous serez de table, accoustemmez vous à laver les
mains avec les autres. Quant à la bouche, il semble
n'estre pas à propos de la laver en présence des
gens, & partant quand l'on donne à laver, mesme en
table, l'on doit seulement laver les mains.
[Maxims, VIII-37]

*Do not rinse your mouth with wine, to be rejected
in the presence of others; but, having left the table,
accustom yourself to wash your hands with the rest. As
to the mouth, it does not appear proper to wash it in
company at all, and consequently when an opportunity
of washing is offered, even at table, the hands only
should be washed.*

102^d: It is out of fashion to call upon the
company, often, to eat; nor need you
drink to others every time you drink.

C'est chose peu loüable & presque aujourd'huy
hors d'usage, d'inviter la compagnie à manger,
principalement trop souvent & avec importunité, car
il semble qu'on luy osté la liberté. Beaucoup moins
devez-vous boire à autruy toutes les fois que vous

boivez. Que si l'on boit à vous, vous pouvez le refuser modestement, rémerciant de bonne grâce, & confessant de vous rendre. Ou bien essayez un peu le vin par courtoisie, principalement avec gens qui sont accoustemez à cela, & prennent le refus à injure. [Maxims, VIII-38]

It is not commendable, and now almost out of fashion, to call on the company to eat, especially to invite them too often and urgently, for it appears to take away their freedom. Much less should you drink to others every time you drink. If one drinks to you, it is permissible to decline modestly, thanking him gracefully and acknowledging your response. Or you may well sip a little wine for courtesy, especially with people who are accustomed to it, and who are offended by refusal.

"Fashion" has been substituted for the word "use" that originally appeared in George Washington's MS version of Rule #102. Giovanni Della Casa counsels that, "if someone should invite you to a drinking bout, you can easily refuse the invitation and say that you admit defeat ... tasting the wine out of courtesy, without drinking more." [*Galateo*, Chap. 29]

Moncure Conway points out the surprising omission from the Washington MS of anything that would follow either the original French Maxims or the later English versions regarding the saying of grace. According to Conway, who was a Unitarian minister, grace was never said before a meal at George Washington's dinner table.

103^d: In the company of your betters, be
          not longer in eating than they are.
          Lay not your arm, but only rest your
          hand on the edge of the table.

Quand les autres ont achevé de manger,
déspechez vous aussi. Ne tenez pas les bras sur la
table, mais posez les mains seulement sur le bout.
[Maxims, VIII-42]

*When the rest have finished eating, you should do
the same quickly. Do not hold your arms on the table,
but only place your hands on the edge of it.*

104th: It belongs to ye chiefest in company
          to unfold his napkin and fall to meat
          first, but he ought to begin in time
          and dispatch with dexterity so that ye
          slowest may have time allowed him.

C'est à faire au plus honnorable de la compagnie
de déplier le premier sa seruiette, & toucher aux
viandes; & partant les autres doivent attendre
paisiblement sans mettre la main à chose aucune
devãt lui. [Maxims, VIII-45]

It is for the most distinguished member of company to be first to unfold his napkin and touch the food, and the rest should wait peacefully, without laying a hand on any of the food before he does.

Et au contraire il doit estre soigneux de commencer en son temps, de pourvoir à tout, d'entretenir les conviez, & finir le tout avec telle addresse, qu'il donne temps aux plus tardifs de manger à leur aise, s'entretenant, s'il est de besoin, à gouster legerement des viandes, ou quand il est loisible de discourir à table, entremesler avec le manger quelque petit discours, afin que les autres puissent avec loisir d'achever. [Maxim, VIII-46]

However, the most distinguished at table must be careful to commence in due time to provide for all, and entertain the guests, managing all of this adroitly, so that late arrivals will have sufficient time to finish their meals with ease, entertaining in the mean time, if that is necessary, slowly tasting the different dishes, or when table-talk is deemed permissible, by introducing light conversation so that the others at table can finish their meal in leisure.

105th: Be not angry at table, whatever happens; and if you have reason to be so, show it not. Put on a cheerful

countenance, especially if there
be strangers, for good humor
makes one dish of meat a feast.

Ne vous fâchez iamais en table, quoy qu'il
advienne, ou bien si vous fâchez, n'ent faites point
de semblant, principalement y ayant des éstrangers à
table. [Maxims, VIII-47]

*Never be angry at table, no matter what may
happen, or even if you have cause for anger, do not
show it, especially if strangers are present.*

A cheerful countenance makes one dish a feast.
[Hawkins, VII-40]

106th: Set not yourself at ye upper end of ye
table, but if it be your due or that ye
master of ye house will have it so.
Contend not, least you should trouble
ye company.

Ne vous asséez point de vous mesme ayu haut-
bout. Mais s'il vous appartient, ou si le maistre du
logis le veut ainsi, ne faites pas tant de resistance
pour n'y point aller, que vous fachiez toute la
compagnie. [Maxims, VIII-48]

Do not seat yourself voluntarily at the head of the table. But if the place properly belongs to you or the master of the house so wills it, do not offer so much resistance to accepting as to annoy the company.

Obadiah Walker puts it a little differently, with: "Desire not the highest place, nor be troublesome with impertinent debasing yourself by refusing."

107th: If others talk at table, be attentive;
         but talk not with meat in your mouth.

Si on lit ou devise en table, soyez attentif, & si'l faut parler, ne parlez point avec le morceau en la bouche. [Maxims, VIII-49]

If there is a reading or some conversation at table, be attentive, and if you have to speak, do not speak with your mouth full.

108th: When you speak of God or His
         attributes, let it be seriously
         and with reverence. Honour
         and obey your natural parents,
         although they may be poor.

Il se faut bien garder de prononcer aucuns nouveaux mots, quand l'on parle de Dieu ou des Saincts, & d'en faire de sots contes, soit tout bon, ou par raillerie. [Maxims, I-9]

Avoid irreverent words in speaking of God or the Saints, and avoid the telling of foolish stories about them, either in jest or in earnest.

... N'employez point de termes bas & ravalez ou populaires en des matières hautes & reluées. [Maxims, VII-11]

... Do not use low, base or vulgar expressions when treating of serious and sublime subjects.

Let thy speeches be seriously reverent when thou speakest of God or his attributes, for to jest or utter thy self lightly in matters divine is an unhappy impiety, provoking Heaven to justice, and urging all men to suspect thy belief. [Hawkins, VII-43]

Honour and obey thy natural parents although they be poor, for if thy earthly parents cannot give thee riches and honour, yet thy heavenly Father hath promised thee length of days. [Hawkins, VII-App.]

As strong evidence that the final three Rules originate in the Hawkins Appendix, it is worth noting that the French Maxims do not contain anything

George Washington's

corresponding to the phrase about honoring one's parents. However, it is equally apparent that the first half of Rule #108 originates in several of the original French Maxims.

109th: Let your recreations be manful,
         and not sinful.

Let thy recreations be manful not sinful. There is a great vanity in the baiting of beasts. The bears and bulls lived quietly enough before the fall; it was our sin that set them together by the ears. Rejoice not therefore to see them fight, for that would be to glory in thy shame. [Hawkins, VII-App.]

110th: Labour to keep alive in your breast
         that little spark of celestial fire
         called conscience.

Labour to keep alive in thy breast that little sparke of Celestial fire called Conscience, for Conscience to an evil man is a never dying worm, but unto a good man it is a perpetual feast. [Hawkins, VII-App.]

~ F I N I S ~

TAKING COMMAND OF THE ARMY.
JULY 12TH 1775.

BIBLIOGRAPHY

Abbot, W.W., ed., *Papers of George Washington*, Univ. Press of Virginia, Charlottesville (1983) Vol. 1.

Anon. [illustrator], *Harper's Weekly*, Harper & Brothers, New York (27 Feby. 1864) Vol. VIII, #374.

Bien-séance de la Conversation entre les Hommes, [or, "Good Manners in Conversation among Men"], Pensionnaires, College of La Flèche, France (1595).

Becker, Marvin B., *Civility and Society in Western Europe ...*, Indiana Univ. Press, Bloomington (1988).

Brookhiser, Richard, *Rules of Civility*, Free Press, New York (1997).

Bryson, Anna, *From Courtesy to Civility: Changing Codes of Conduct ...*, Clarendon Press, Oxford (1998).

Bushman, Richard L., *The Refinement of America*, Alfred A. Knopf, New York (1992).

Castiglione, Baldassare, *Il libro del Cortegiano*, Venetia (1528); *Book of the Courtier*, London (1561).

Codrington, Robert, ... *Decency in Conversation amongst Women*, W. Lee, London (1664).

Conway, Moncure D., *George Washington's Rules of Civility, traced to their sources ...*, Hurst & Co., New York (1890); Chatto & Windus, London (1890).

Courtin, Antoine de, *Nouveau traité de la civilité*, Paris (1670); *The Rules of Civility* [English trans.], J. Martyn & John Starkey, London (1671, 1675, 1678).

Cushing, Stanley Ellis, *The George Washington Library Collection*, Boston Athenaeum, Boston (1997).

della Casa, Giovanni, *Il Galateo*, Venice (1558); *Treatise of Manners*, Robert Peterson [trans.], London (1576); *Galateo*, Konrad Eisenbichler & Kenneth Bartlett [trans.], Victoria Univ. Press, Toronto (1986).

Dictionary of National Biography [UK], Smith, Elder & Co., London (1891-1899) Vols. XXV & LIX.

Elias, Norbert, *The History of Manners*, (1939); Edmund Jephcott [trans.], Urizen, New York (1978).

Erasmus, Desiderius, *De civilitate morum puerilium*, Coloniae (1530); Robert Whytyngton [English trans.], Wynkyn de Worde, London (1532).

Fisher, George, *The Instructor; or Young Man's Best Companion*, London (1727); James Hodges, London (5th Edition, 1740; 13th Edition, 1755).

Ford, Worthington Chauncey, *Inventory of the Contents of Mount Vernon*, Mt. Vernon (1801, 1909).

Foyster, Elizabeth A., *Manhood in Early Modern England: Honour ...*, Longman, Ltd., London (1999).

Green, Charles [illustrator], *The Graphic: An Illustrated Weekly Newspaper*, London (1881, 1882).

Griffin, Appleton P.C., *Catalogue of the Washington Collection in the Boston Athenaeum* [an index], John Wilson & Son, Cambridge Mass. (1900).

Hawkins, Francis [trans.], *Youth's Behaviour, or Decency in Conversation amongst men ...*, W. Wilson, London (1641, 1646, 1651, 1654, 1663, 1672).

Hemphill, C. Dallett, *Bowing to Necessities: A History of Manners ...*, Oxford Press, New York (1999).

Huguet, Edmond, *Dictionnaire de la Langue Française du Siezieme Siecle*, Paris (1925-1967) 7 Vols.

Irving, Washington, *Life of George Washington*, (1855); Sleepy Hollow, Tarrytown (abridged, 1975).

Johnson, Samuel, *Dictionary of the English Language*, London (1755); Alex. Chalmers [editor], Studio Editions, Ltd., London (abridged, 1843, 1994).

Knollenberg, Bernhard, *George Washington: The Virginia Period, 1732-1775*, Duke Press, Durham (1964).

Mason, John E., *Gentlefolk in the Making*, Univ. of Pennsylvania Press, Philadelphia (1935).

Mitchell, S. Weir, M.D., *The Youth of Washington*, The Century Company, New York (1904).

Moody, Eleazar, *The School of Good Manners*, T. Green, New London (1715); Fifth Edition, (1754).

Moore, Charles, *George Washington's Rules of Civility* ..., Houghton Mifflin Co., New York (1926).

Nitzman, Joannes, *Communis vitae inter homines scita urbanitas*, Pawla Gesse, Leta (1629).

Peacham, Henry, *The Compleat Gentleman*, F. Constable, London (1622); J. Legate, London (1634).

Périn, Léonard, *Les Maximes de la Gentillesse et de l'Honnesteté en la Conversation ordinaire entre les Hommes*, Pont-à-Mousson (1617); Paris (1638); Rouen (1651); G. Lee [Latin trans.], Londini (1652, 1663); revised, Pierre de Bresche [Latin & French trans.], College de Clermont, Paris (1663).

Rasmussen, William M.S. and Tilton, Robert S., *George Washington: The Man Behind the Myths*, Univ. Press of Virginia, Charlottesville (1999).

Sayen, William Guthrie, "George Washington's 'Unmannerly' Behaviour," *Virginia Magazine of History & Biography*, Richmond (1999) Vol. 107:1, pp. 5-36.

Schroeder, John Frederick, *Maxims of Washington*, D. Appleton & Co., New York (1855).

Sparks, Jared [editor], *The Writings of George Washington*, Ferdinand Andrews, Boston (1839).

Stoddard, William, *George Washington's Fifty-seven Rules of Behaviour*, W.H. Lawrence, Denver (1886).

Twohig, Dorothy, "... The Papers of George Washington," *Virginia Cavalcade*, Library of Virginia, Richmond (1999) Vol. 48:4, pp. 148-157.

Walker, Obadiah, *Of Education. Especially of Young Gentlemen*, At the theatre, Oxon (1673); Richard Wellington, London (1699); Amos Custeyne, Oxford (1887); Scholar Press, Menston (1970).

Warren, Jack D., Jr., "The Childhood of George Washington," *Northern Neck of Virginia Historical Magazine*, Montross (1999) XLIX:1, pp. 5785-5809.

Washington, George, *George Washington's Rules of Civility & Decent Behaviour* ..., J.M. Toner [editor], W.H. Morrison, Washington, D.C. (1888); revised, Mt. Vernon Ladies' Assoc., Mt. Vernon (1989, 2002).

Washington, George, *Papers*, Library of Congress: http://lcweb2.loc.gov/ammem/gwhtml/gwhome.html and Univ. of Virginia: www.virginia.edu/gwpapers

Whipple, Wayne, *The Story of Young George Washington*, Henry Altemus Co., Philadelphia (1915).

Who Was Who, 1897-1915 [Conway, Moncure], A. & C. Black, London (1988).

SUBJECT INDEX

Academics	Rule 61
Advice & criticism:	
giving	Rules 18, 41, 45, 47, 48, 65, 68-70, 83
taking	Rule 46, 86
Affectations:	
avoiding	Rules 19, 25-27, 31, 36, 52, 54
invoking	Rules 22, 32, 45, 46, 83, 105
Anger, avoiding	Rule 45, 49, 58, 83, 105
Arguments, avoiding	Rules 34, 40, 69, 87, 106
Arrogance, avoiding	Rules 36, 41, 54, 61, 106
Artisans, mentioned	Rule 36
Bad company	Rule 56
Beard, pulling on	Rule 16
Bed, making yours	Rule 7
Belching, avoid	Rule 99
Biting lips or nails	Rules 11, 16
Blemishes, noticing	Rule 71
Brave acts, honoring	Rule 78
Business:	
conduct of	Rules 35, 41, 44, 45, 77, 82
privacy	Rules 18, 77, 81, 83, 84
Celestial fire	Rule 110
Center of attention	Rule 57
Ceremony:	
attending to	Rules 25, 42, 104
placement at	Rules 27, 106
Chamber-maids	Rule 72

Circumspection	Rule 68
Cleanliness, generally	Rules 15, 51, 96, 101
Clothing:	
appropriate	Rules 7, 52, 54
doffing hat	Rules 26, 27, 85
cleaning &etc.	Rules 13, 51
Comparisons, avoid	Rule 78
Compliments	Rules 17, 35
Composure	Rules 8, 12, 19, 24, 45, 47, 51, 53, 58, 64, 73, 76, 83, 87, 91, 99, 105
Conduct, in company:	
associations	Rule 56
bowing	Rule 26
clothing	Rules 7, 51, 52, 54
facial expression	Rules 12, 16, 19, 35, 53
flattery	Rules 17, 25, 35
generally	Rules 1, 6, 27, 59, 77, 105
grooming	Rule 15
as host	Rules 31, 32, 104, 106
as office-holder	Rule 33
reading	Rules 18, 80
respect for others	Rules 1, 3, 6, 14, 33, 71, 75, 78
sitting	Rules 6, 10, 27, 28, 32
speaking	Rules 6, 14, 37, 39, 46, 49, 73, 76, 77, 80, 85, 88, 98
stretching	Rule 11
walking	Rules 6, 30, 31, 53, 57
Conduct, private acts:	
"adjusting"	Rules 2, 11, 90
reprimands	Rules 45, 46, 48, 49, 67, 70
with the sick	Rules 38, 43
undressing	Rule 7

Conduct, public acts:
composure	Rules 8, 45, 66, 83, 91, 99
coughing	Rules 5, 90
at fireplace	Rule 9
generally	Rules 4, 9, 13, 23, 33, 54
killing vermin	Rule 13
laughing	Rules 24, 47, 64, 84
office-holders	Rule 33
at punishment	Rule 23
reading	Rules 18, 80
respect for others	Rules 1, 6, 29, 33, 67, 71, 75, 78
scratching	Rules 2, 90
singing, humming	Rule 4
sneezing	Rule 5, 90
speaking	Rules 6, 14, 39, 49, 65, 73, 76, 85, 98
walking	Rules 29, 30, 53, 57
Confidence	Rule 79
Conscience	Rule 110

Conversation:
consider audience	Rules 25, 61, 75, 105
consider setting	Rules 62, 77, 105
decorum	Rules 6, 12, 14, 18, 19, 37, 43, 74, 76, 83, 85, 87, 89
generally	Rules 17, 34, 35, 40, 58, 66, 69, 78, 89
interruptions	Rules 74, 75, 84
listening, in	Rules 41, 66, 74, 85-87, 107
precision, in	Rules 35, 61, 68, 73, 77, 80, 85, 88
proper language	Rules 42, 49, 58, 59, 72, 89
proper subjects	Rules 61, 62, 77, 87

Coughing   Rules 5, 90
Courtesy, place for   Rules 13, 31, 32, 36, 42,
                               67, 74, 78
Criminals punished   Rule 23
Cursing, improper   Rules 49, 59, 72
Decorum, regarding:
  business   Rules 18, 35, 41, 45, 77, 83
  church   Rule 53
  fireplace   Rules 8, 9
  infirmities   Rules 21, 70, 71
  misfortune   Rules 22, 64
  public spectacles   Rules 23, 24, 53, 54
  sickness   Rules 38, 43
Deference, giving   Rules 34, 40-42, 46, 69, 86
Desks, generally   Rules 7, 14
Digressions   Rule 88
Distance, proper   Rules 12, 14, 18, 37, 51, 76, 81
Doorway, yielding in   Rule 29
Dreams, sharing   Rule 62
Eating & drinking   (see "Table manners")
Eating between meals   Rule 55
Enemies, treating   Rules 22, 65, 67, 89
Elbows, generally   Rules 51, 91, 103
Envy, avoiding   Rule 58
Exhortations   Rule 45
Facial expressions   Rules 12, 16, 19, 35
Feet, use of   Rules 4, 9, 10, 53
Fidgeting, avoid   Rules 12, 15
Fingers, misusing   Rules 4, 76, 96
Fireplace, etiquette   Rules 8, 9
Flattery   Rules 17, 25, 35
Fleas, ticks, &etc.   Rules 13, 51
Gestures   Rules 20, 76

Gluttony, avoiding	Rules 91, 97
God, revering	Rule 108
Gossip	Rules 58, 65, 79, 81, 89
Gravity, required	Rules 19, 47, 64, 72
Greeting	Rules 26, 28, 66
Grooming	Rules 13, 15
Habits, forming	Rule 2
Handkerchief, use of	Rules 5, 54, 90
Hats, doffing	Rules 26, 27, 85
Hosting	Rules 28, 31, 32, 93, 104, 106
Humility	Rule 63
Infirmities	Rules 21, 38, 43, 70, 71
Interrupting, avoid	Rules 74, 75, 84, 86, 107
Joking, on others	Rules 3, 17, 47, 64, 65
"Keep your promise"	Rule 82
Killing vermin	Rule 13
Kindness, practicing	Rules 3, 13, 21, 36, 43, 89
Laughing	Rules 24, 47, 64, 84
"Lead by example"	Rules 48, 59
Lips, pursing, wiping	Rules 16, 99
Listening, need for	Rules 41, 66, 74, 85-87, 107
Majority, following	Rule 86 (see "Deference")
"Make your bed"	Rule 7
Malice, avoiding	Rules 58, 65, 83, 89
Mediating disputes	Rules 69, 86
Medicine, bad	Rule 38
Misfortune	Rule 22, 44, 64
Modesty	Rules 15, 32, 33, 40, 47, 52, 54, 60, 63, 67, 72
Mother tongue	Rules 72, 77
Name-calling	Rule 65
New-comers, welcome	Rules 8, 68
Night-cap, place for	Rule 7

Noises, making	Rule 99
Office-holders	Rule 33
Opinions, offering	Rules 40, 41, 45, 68, 69, 86
Parents, role/ honor	Rules 70, 108
Patrons	Rule 86
Playing	Rule 8
"Play not a peacock"	Rules 15, 52, 54
Posture	Rules 10, 11, 20, 85
Practical jokes	Rules 17, 64
Preach, when not to	Rules 41, 69
Pretensions, avoid	Rules 38, 52, 54, 61, 82
Privacy:	
obtaining	Rules 18, 45, 71, 77, 83
respect for	Rules 18, 60, 79, 81, 83, 84
Private parts	Rules 2, 11
Promises, keeping	Rule 82
Quarrels, avoiding	Rules 87, 106
"Rank has privilege"	Rules 6, 9, 18, 28, 32, 33, 34, 37, 39, 40, 42, 57, 75, 103, 104, 106
Rashness, avoid	Rule 41, 50
Reading in public	Rules 18, 80
Recreations, manful	Rule 109
Repartee	Rule 47
Repetition, avoiding	Rule 88
Reprimands	Rules 44-46, 48, 49, 67, 70
Reputation, guarding	Rules 50, 56, 58, 82
Respect for:	
local customs	Rules 26, 27, 30, 39, 52, 102
the infirm/ sick	Rules 21, 38, 43, 71
others, generally	Rules 1, 3, 6, 14, 21, 31, 33, 44, 45, 67, 74-78, 83, 86, 89, 99, 104

Respect for:
  privacy   Rules 18, 60, 79, 81, 83, 84
  superiors   Rules 26, 27, 29, 30, 33, 34,
                              36, 37, 39, 40, 57, 70, 75,
                              84, 85, 103, 104, 106, 108

Rumors - caution   Rules 50, 61, 65, 79, 89
Saluting   Rules 26, 27, 29, 66
Seating, rank in   Rules 28, 32, 33, 106
Secrets, keeping   Rules 60, 62, 71, 77, 79
Servants, mentioned   Rules 8, 9, 27, 59, 72
"Short & sweet ..."   Rules 35, 61, 68, 80, 88
Sickness   Rules 38, 43
Sighs, controlling   Rule 5
Sitting, generally   Rules 6, 10, 27, 28, 32, 51
Sneezing, in public   Rule 5
Speaking:
  generally   Rules 6, 12, 39, 42, 59, 72-75,
                              98, 107, 108
  using gestures   Rules 20, 76
  "when spoken to"   Rule 85
  with superiors   Rules 34, 37, 40, 75, 84, 85
Spitting/ spittle   Rules 9, 12, 13, 90, 95
Stretching   Rule 11
Table manners:
  bite-size pieces   Rules 91, 94, 97
  conversation   Rules 62, 91, 105, 107
  drinking   Rules 98, 99, 102
  elbows, place for   Rules 91, 103
  etiquette, generally   Rules 90, 92, 95, 98, 102-107
  fruit pits   Rule 95
  "good humor makes ... a feast"   Rule 105
  as guest   Rule 93, 106
  as host   Rules 93, 104-106

Table manners:
    knife, use of   Rules 91, 92, 95, 100
    moderation   Rules 91, 94, 96-99
    making noises   Rule 99
    rinsing out mouth   Rule 101
    soup, blowing on   Rule 94
    table napkin, use   Rules 96, 99, 100, 104
    where & when   Rules 55, 103, 104
Teeth, generally   Rules 15, 100, 101
Tedium, avoiding   Rule 80
"Thank you," saying   Rule 13
Thinking:
    before acting   Rule 45, 58, 67, 83
    before speaking   Rule 46, 49, 58, 65, 73, 87
"Timing is everything"   Rules 55, 77, 103, 104
Toasting   Rule 102
Truth, regarding   Rule 79
Undressing   Rule 7
Virtue   Rules 63, 78
Visiting   Rules 68, 93
Walking:
    generally   Rule 53
    place, by rank   Rules 6, 29-31, 33, 57
Welcome, newcomers Rules 8, 68
"When in Rome ..."   Rules 26, 27, 30, 39, 52, 102
Whispering, avoid   Rules 72, 77
Wine   Rules 91, 99, 101, 102
Wisdom   Rule 40
Wit, exercising   Rule 47
Working, decorum   Rules 7, 9
Writing, letters   Rules 14, 39
Yawning, in company Rule 5